# DK EYEWITNESS

T0047002

# TOP 10
# DELHI

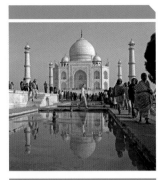

# Top 10 Delhi Highlights

Welcome to Delhi............................**5**

Exploring Delhi...............................**6**

Delhi Highlights ...........................**10**

Red Fort.........................................**12**

Chandni Chowk............................**14**

Jama Masjid..................................**16**

Humayun's Tomb.........................**18**

Around Kartavya Path..................**20**

Qutb Minar Complex....................**24**

National Crafts Museum.............**28**

Lodi Gardens................................**30**

National Museum .........................**32**

Taj Mahal, Agra and
    Fatehpur Sikri...........................**36**

# The Top 10 of Everything

Moments in History .....................**42**

Delhi Sultanate Sights................**44**

Mughal Delhi Sights ....................**46**

Monuments of the
    1857 Uprising...........................**48**

Cities of Delhi,
    Old and New.............................**50**

Places of Worship .......................**52**

Museums and Galleries .............**54**

Delhi-Inspired Books..................**56**

Parks and Gardens ......................**58**

Off the Beaten Track...................**60**

Performing Arts Venues.............**62**

Places to Eat ................................**64**

Bazaars of Old Delhi...................**66**

Delhi for Free ...............................**68**

Festivals and Events ...................**70**

Excursions from Delhi................**72**

# CONTENTS

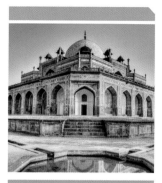

## Delhi
## Area by Area

New Delhi......................................**76**

Old Delhi......................................**84**

South of the Centre.....................**92**

South Delhi..................................**98**

## Streetsmart

Getting Around............................**108**

Practical Information.................**110**

Places to Stay............................**114**

General Index.............................**120**

Acknowledgments.....................**126**

Selected Street Index................**128**

Within each Top 10 list in this book, no hierarchy of quality or popularity is implied. All 10 are, in the editor's opinion, of roughly equal merit.

***Title page, front cover and spine***
*The Khas Mahal in the Red Fort*
***Back cover, clockwise from top left***
*Spices in a local bazaar; India Gate at twilight; Busy Paharganj area; Khas Mahal, Red Fort; Qutb Minar at sunset*

The rapid rate at which the world is changing is constantly keeping the DK Eyewitness team on our toes. While we've worked hard to ensure that this edition of Delhi is accurate and up-to-date, we know that opening hours alter, standards shift, prices fluctuate, places close and new ones pop up in their stead. So, if you notice we've got something wrong or left something out, we want to hear about it. Please get in touch at **travelguides@dk.com**

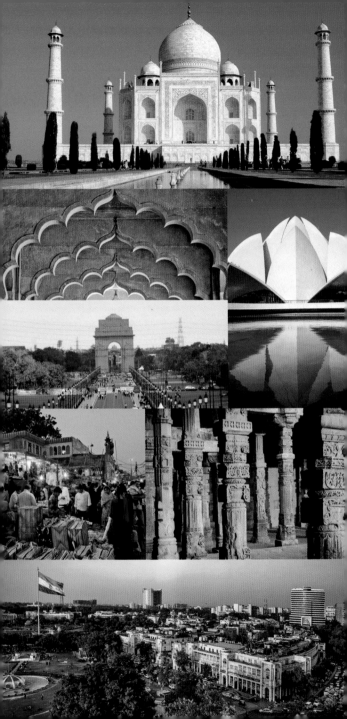

# Welcome to
# Delhi

India's capital and seat of power presents a dynamic mix of past and present. Studded with exquisite Mughal-era relics, grand imperial avenues, intriguing museums and world-famous bazaars, this gleaming metropolis is a riot of vibrant colour and noise. With DK Eyewitness Top 10 Delhi, it's yours to explore.

At the heart of the capital is **New Delhi**, the British-built imperial city: elegant and spacious, with fine dining and excellent shopping, bisected by the wide thoroughfare known as **Kartavya Path**. The 17th-century Mughal city of **Old Delhi**, by contrast, is a warren of teeming bazaars concealing all manner of fascinating nooks and crannies, but its magnificent constructions – the famous **Red Fort** complex and the **Jama Masjid** among them – are just as impressive as those of the new city.

**South of the centre**, the **garden tombs of Humayun and Safdarjung** put into context that zenith of Mughal architecture: the **Taj Mahal** in **Agra**, an easy excursion from Delhi, along with the long-abandoned but architecturally rich Mughal city of **Fatehpur Sikri**. Meanwhile, Delhi's modern, efficient and ever-expanding metro system puts the scattered sights of **South Delhi** into easy reach – most notably the 12th-century **Qutb Minar**, which marks the original location of one of the older seven cities of Delhi – before heading out to the satellite towns of **Noida** and **Gurugram** (Gurgaon), burgeoning IT hubs that crackle with the dynamism of an up-and-coming new India.

Whether you're visiting for a weekend or a week, our Top 10 guide brings together the best of everything that Delhi has to offer, from the hottest Indian cuisine to the most magnificent monuments. The guide has useful tips throughout, from seeking out what's free to places off the beaten track, plus six easy-to-follow itineraries, designed to tie together a clutch of sights in a short space of time. Add inspiring photography and detailed maps, and you've got the essential pocket-sized travel companion. **Enjoy the book, and enjoy Delhi**.

Clockwise from top: Taj Mahal, Baha'i Lotus Temple, pillars in the Qutb Minar complex, Connaught Place, Meena Bazaar, Kartavya Path leading to India Gate, detail from the Red Fort

# Exploring Delhi

There are so many sights to see and things to do in Delhi, you could easily spend a couple of weeks here. Whether you're visiting for a weekend or have the luxury of an extra couple of days, these two- and four-day itineraries will help you make the most of your time in this vibrant city.

**The Red Fort** offers a glimpse into the opulent lifestyle of the city's former rulers.

## Two Days in Delhi

### Day ❶
**MORNING**
From **Khari Baoli** *(see p66)* market, take a stroll or a cycle-rickshaw down **Chandni Chowk** *(see pp14–15)* to the **Red Fort** *(see pp12–13)*, before going to see the **Jama Masjid** *(see pp16–17)*.

**AFTERNOON**
Take an auto-rickshaw to the **National Crafts Museum** *(see pp28–9)*, then take a short walk to **Purana Qila** *(see p93)*. From there head to **Humayun's Tomb** *(see pp18–19)* and **Nizamuddin** *(see pp94–5)*.

### Day ❷
**MORNING**
Start at **Gandhi Smriti** *(see p79)* and from there walk or take an auto-rickshaw to **Safdarjung's Tomb** *(see p94)*. Later, go for a stroll around the peaceful **Lodi Gardens** *(see pp30–31)*.

**AFTERNOON**
Take an auto-rickshaw along **Kartavya Path** *(see pp20–21)* from **Rashtrapati Bhavan** to **India Gate** and then head to the **National Museum** *(see pp32–5)*. After, ride the metro from Udyog Bhawan station to visit the fascinating red sandstone **Qutb Minar** *(see pp24–7)* complex.

## Four Days in Delhi

### Day ❶
**MORNING**
See the **Red Fort** *(see pp12–13)*, then pop into the **Lal Mandir** *(see p87)* and **Gauri Shankar Mandir** *(see p88)* before walking down **Chandni Chowk** to the **Fatehpuri Masjid** *(see p15)* and **Khari Baoli** *(see p66)* market.

**AFTERNOON**
Take a rickshaw to **Qudsia Bagh** *(see p88)*, then check out **Nicholson's Cemetery** *(see p49)* and the **Kashmiri Gate** *(see p49)* before heading past

0 metres 1000
0 yards 1000

ritish
esidency

Red
Fort

AUTO-RICKSHAW

National Crafts
Museum

tional
r
morial

Purana
Qila

AUTO-RICKSHAW

Humayun's
Tomb

Agra,
Fatephur Sikri
210 km (130 miles)

Nizamuddin

**Key**
— Two-day itinerary
— Four-day itinerary

**The Taj Mahal**, Shah Jahan's sublime mausoleum, is a
magnificent example of Mughal architecture.

**Safdarjung's
Tomb** features
this beautifully
decorated arch
just above the
main entrance.

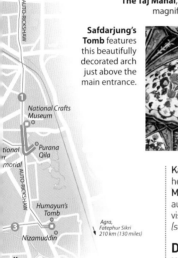

St James' Church (see p85) and the
British Residency (see p48) with a
cycle-rickshaw to the Jama Masjid
(see pp16–17), finishing with a mutton
korma at Karim's (see p65).

## Day ❷
**MORNING**
From Connaught Place (see p77),
head to the Jantar Mantar (see p78),
then take an auto across Kartavya
Path (see pp20–21) to the National
Museum (see pp32–5).
**AFTERNOON**
Get an auto-rickshaw to Rashtrapati
Bhavan (see p21), then another along

Kartavya Path to India Gate. From
here walk to the National War
Memorial (see p20) and then get an
auto to Purana Qila (see p93). Next,
visit the National Crafts Museum
(see pp28–9).

## Day ❸
**MORNING**
Start at the Qutb Minar (see pp24–7),
visit the Mehrauli Archaeological
Park (see pp26–27), then take the
metro to Safdarjung's Tomb (see p94).
**AFTERNOON**
Visit Gandhi Smriti (see p79) before
exploring the Lodi Gardens (see
pp30–31). Then, head to Humayun's
Tomb (see pp18–19) and the dargah
in Nizamuddin (see pp94–5).

## Day ❹
**MORNING**
Take the morning train to Agra and
visit the Taj Mahal (see pp36–7).
**AFTERNOON**
Get a taxi to Fatehpur Sikri (see p39),
before returning to Agra in time to
catch the evening train back to Delhi.

# Top 10 Delhi Highlights

An icon of India, the Taj Mahal
in Agra, Uttar Pradesh

| | | | |
|---|---|---|---|
| Delhi Highlights | 10 | Qutb Minar Complex | 24 |
| Red Fort | 12 | National Crafts Museum | 28 |
| Chandni Chowk | 14 | Lodi Gardens | 30 |
| Jama Masjid | 16 | National Museum | 32 |
| Humayun's Tomb | 18 | Taj Mahal, Agra and Fatehpur Sikri | 36 |
| Around Kartavya Path | 20 | | |

# 🔟 Delhi Highlights

History is writ large in Delhi, and few places in the world can rival the city's incredible clutch of monuments, spanning 1,000 years of history. These range from the soaring minaret of the Qutb Minar and the imposing Red Fort to the dramatic Jama Masjid and Humayun's Tomb, as well as some of the most grandiose landmarks of the British Raj, such as India Gate.

### Red Fort

A former residence of the powerful Mughal emperors, the enormous Red Fort is Old Delhi's iconic showpiece attraction, providing a fascinating peek into the cultured world of the country's most charismatic rulers *(see pp12–13)*.

### ② Chandni Chowk

At the heart of Old Delhi, this famous Mughal thoroughfare, lined with mosques, temples and myriad shops, offers a colourful slice of quintessential Indian street life *(see pp14–15)*.

### Jama Masjid ③

The largest and most spectacular mosque in India, this Mughal monument rises out of the streets of Old Delhi *(see pp16–17)*.

### ④ Humayun's Tomb

The first of the great Mughal garden tombs, this is one of ancient Delhi's most beautiful historical monuments *(see pp18–19)*.

### ⑤ Kartavya Path

As the centrepiece of imperial Delhi, this Raj-era thoroughfare is a lasting example of colonial pomp, stretching from the stately India Gate to the grand Rashtrapati Bhavan *(see pp20–21)*.

### 6 Qutb Minar Complex

Towering over southern Delhi, the Qutb Minar is perhaps the city's single most dramatic sight, surrounded by monuments from the Sultanate and Mughal periods (see pp24–5).

### National Crafts Museum 7

This museum offers a fascinating snapshot of local arts-and-crafts traditions of the subcontinent, from arcane religious artifacts to traditional village houses (see pp28–9).

### 8 Lodi Gardens

The idyllic Lodi Gardens are dotted with a sequence of atmospheric tombs built in honour of the Delhi sultans. The landscaped grounds make them ideal for a picnic (see pp30–31).

### 9 National Museum

The National Museum is India's finest, with an enormous collection of artifacts and exhibits ranging from the Indus Valley Civilization to the 20th century, covering every aspect of the country's varied cultural history (see pp32–5).

### Taj Mahal 10

Perhaps the most famous – and certainly the most beautiful – monument in the world, the incomparable Taj Mahal in Agra, a masterpiece of Mughal architecture is a day-trip away from Delhi (see pp36–7).

# TOP 10 ★ Red Fort

In 1638, the Mughal emperor Shah Jahan (r 1628–58) decided to leave Agra, then capital of the empire, and return to Delhi. Here he established Shahjahanabad, or Old Delhi as it is now known, with the Red Fort (Lal Quila) at its heart. The structure was completed in 1648 and surrounded by enormous red sandstone walls, their colour lending the fort its name. It served as home to the emperor and his successors until the 1857 Uprising. Although time has taken its toll, it remains one of Delhi's most absorbing sights.

**1 Naqqar Khana**
The second of the fort's major gateways, the Naqqar (or Naubat) Khana was where all visitors were obliged to dismount from their elephants to enter the inner court. In the gallery above, musicians would perform in welcome.

**2 Khas Mahal**
The emperor's lavishly decorated private apartments are divided by a marble latticework screen surmounted by the scales of justice.

**3 Hayat Bakhsh Bagh**
North of the Moti Masjid lies the Hayat Bakhsh Bagh, or Life-Bestowing Garden, with two small marble pavilions **(below)** at either end, and the pretty Zafar Mahal, a red sandstone pavilion, in a pool in the middle.

**4 Moti Masjid**
Built in 1659, the Moti Masjid is closed to visitors, though visitors can peer through its latticed marble screens for a glimpse of the delicate courtyard within.

**Red Fort map**

### 5 Lahori Gate

The Red Fort's main entrance is the majestic Lahori Gate **(left)**, although its original grandeur has been obscured by the bastion added by Aurangzeb (1618–1707), designed to force attackers into a sideways approach.

### 6 Diwan-i-Khas

This pillared hall is where the emperor would have conferred with his ministers on affairs of state; it was also where Emperor Shah Jahan's legendary, jewel-encrusted Peacock Throne was housed. It remains easily the most lavish building in the fort, with fine marble carving and *pietra dura* inlay work.

### 7 Diwan-i-Aam

One of the Red Fort's most impressive structures, this very elegant sandstone pavilion **(left)** is where the emperor used to hold his public audiences.

**THE RED FORT IN THE AGE OF THE MUGHALS**

Impressive as it is, what visitors see of the Red Fort today is only a part of the original structure, once a veritable city within a city, with lovely pavilions and gracious courtyards, many of which, sadly, have now vanished. Much of the blame for this falls on the British, who, after the 1857 Uprising, razed many of the fort's grand buildings to the ground. They erected a rather overbearing sequence of barracks in their place which, unfortunately, survive to this day.

### 9 Shahi Burj and Burj-i-Shamali

The Shahi Burj tower is where water was drawn from the Yamuna River for use within the fort. Aurangzeb later added a fine marble pavilion, called the Burj-i-Shamli, with a water chute leading to a scalloped basin.

**NEED TO KNOW**

**MAP H3** ■ Chandni Chowk ■ Lal Quila Metro; Chandni Chowk Metro ■ https://asi.nic.in/red-fort-delhi

**Open** 9:30am–4:30pm Tue–Sun; Jai Hind sound and light show: 8:15–9:15pm Tue–Fri

Adm ₹600 (Indians ₹50), video ₹25, audio guides ₹100 plus tax and deposit

■ Take a short break at the café and visit Kranti Mandir, a complex of museums located in the fort premises.

### 8 Rang Mahal

The centre of the Red Fort's women's quarters **(above)** has carved marble walls, an inlaid marble fountain and the remains of ornate mirrorwork on the ceiling.

### 10 Salimgarh Fort

North of the Red Fort is Salimgarh, built in 1546 and later used by the British to imprison independence fighters. It now houses a museum.

# ⭐ Chandni Chowk

When Shah Jahan built his new city, Chandni Chowk was planned as its principal thoroughfare – a broad, ceremonial avenue leading directly from the Red Fort and a favoured spot for elaborate processions. Most of the street's original buildings are now gone (along with the canal which ran down the middle of the road), but Chandni Chowk, lined with shoebox shops, and eternally bustling with crowds and traffic, retains much of its traditional atmosphere.

### ① Gurudwara Sisganj
This large, modern Sikh temple **(above)** commemorates the spot where the ninth Sikh guru, Teg Bahadur, was beheaded on the orders of Mughal emperor Aurangzeb in 1675.

### ② Bhai Mati Dass Museum
The museum provides a comprehensive history of the Sikhs in pictures, including some portraits of the ten Sikh gurus.

### ③ Lal Mandir
Built during the reign of Shah Jahan for the Jain traders he invited to settle here, the Lal Mandir (Red Temple) is one of Delhi's principal Jain shrines. The temple's red towers are major landmarks at the fort end of Chandni Chowk.

### ④ Town Hall
The elegant British Town Hall **(below)** built in 1864, stands out from cluttered buildings of Chandni Chowk.

**NEED TO KNOW**

**MAP G3** ▪ Chandni Chowk Metro; Lal Quila Metro

▪ A rickshaw ride is a fun way to experience the main stretch of the busy market between the historic Red Fort and Fatehpuri Masjid. This is a "no-traffic zone" for motorized vehicles between 9am and 9pm.

▪ Head to Haldiram's *(see p89)* for a light meal, or get a tasty *parantha* from the Paranthe Wali Gali *(see p89)*.

**Narrow streets lined with shops in Chandni Chowk**

### CHAINA RAM

Sadly, Chandni Chowk's most famous sweet shop, Ghantewala, established in 1790, closed in 2015. But sweet lovers won't go hungry, because at the street's western end, Chaina Ram, founded in Karachi in 1901, makes the best halwa in India. Its Hindu owner was forced to flee Pakistan in 1947, but in what amounts to a statement against sectarianism, he set up shop in a Muslim neighbourhood.

### 9 Begum Samru's Palace

Half-buried in the middle of a crowded bazaar just off the main street, this huge Neo-Classical mansion (now occupied by the Central Bank of India), was once one of the grandest buildings in Delhi. It was built back in 1823, and had gardens which stretched all the way to Chandni Chowk.

### 5 Sunehri Masjid

This small Mughal mosque (1721) was named for its gilded domes (*sunehri* meaning "golden"). It was from here that Persian invader Nadir Shah watched his soldiers massacre the city's inhabitants in 1739.

### 7 Central Baptist Church

The first Christian mission in northern India when it was founded in 1814 (although the current building dates from 1858), this modest church is an atmospheric memento of the Raj era.

### 10 Fatehpuri Masjid

Located at the far west end of Chandni Chowk, the Fatehpuri Masjid **(below)** was built by a wife of Shah Jahan in 1650, and has an enormous and wonderfully peaceful courtyard.

### 6 Gauri Shankar Mandir

Created for Shankar (Shiva) and Gauri (his wife Parvati), this vibrant Hindu temple features an ancient *lingam*, a symbol of worship of the god Shiva; it is said to be around 800 years old.

### 8 Lala Chunna Mal's Haveli

Built by Hindu merchant Lala Chunna Mal, who had made a fortune supplying British forces in the 1857 Uprising, this sprawling, balconied mansion has no fewer than 128 rooms.

# 🔟 ⭐ Jama Masjid

Completed in 1656, the Jama Masjid (Friday Mosque, named after the Muslim day of prayer) is the largest mosque in India, with three huge domes, a pair of minarets over 40 m (131 ft) tall and a courtyard large enough to hold 25,000 worshippers. The mosque is an architectural masterpiece and took six years to build, using 5,000 masons and at a cost of around a million rupees. Today, its soaring minarets and domes are among Old Delhi's most memorable sights.

**1 The Façade**
The prayer hall's façade **(above)** is the most impressive of any Indian mosque. Ten cusped arches flank the central *iwan* (main arch), indicating the direction of Mecca and providing a focus of prayer to the many worshippers.

**Jama Masjid map**

**2 The Eastern Approach**
The most dramatic approach to Jama Masjid is from the east, between the busy stalls of the Meena Bazaar, with the grand mosque looming ahead.

**3 Meena Bazaar**
This busy market on the eastern approach sells prayer rugs, framed Koranic inscriptions, kufi caps and other Islamic items **(left)**, amid the smoky scent of freshly cooked kebabs from the dozens of nearby *dhabas*.

**4 Tomb of Maulana Azad**
Halfway along Meena Bazaar, an opening on the right leads up to a raised tomb that houses the remains of Maulana Azad (1888–1958), a major figure in the fight for Indian independence.

### ⑥ Prayer Hall
On the western side of the courtyard is the enormous *liwan*, or prayer hall. Its western wall is punctuated by no fewer than seven *mihrabs*, niches that indicate the direction of Mecca to worshippers. A graceful *minbar*, or pulpit, stands to the right.

### ⑦ The Courtyard
Designed as a place to go for communal worship, the enormous, breezy courtyard **(below)** has space for thousands of religious worshippers.

> **SHAH JAHAN: MASTER BUILDER**
>
> Mughal emperor Shah Jahan was a prolific builder, who during his 30-year reign, promoted an architectural outpouring that has never been matched. In addition to Delhi's Jama Masjid and the Red Fort, he commissioned extensive additions to the Agra Fort (*see p38*), and oversaw a spate of construction in Lahore, Pakistan (including the Shalimar Gardens), not to mention the superb Taj Mahal (*see pp36–7*).

### ⑨ South Minaret Views
The South Minaret affords unrivalled views **(below)** of Old Delhi. There are about 120 narrow steps and not much space at the top.

### ⑤ The Minarets
The main prayer hall is framed by two brick minarets topped with *chhatris* (pavilions). Their slender outlines add a lightness to the long, arcaded façade, with its three bulbous marble domes.

### ⑧ Pataudi House Mosque
This is one of Delhi's prettiest little mosques – white with triple domes and frilly doorways. It dates as far back as the 18th century, when it was part of a *haveli*, that is now long gone.

**NEED TO KNOW**

MAP H4 ■ Off Netaji Subhash Marg ■ 011 2336 5358 ■ Chawri Bazaar Metro; Jama Masjid Metro

**Open** 7am–noon & 1:30–6:30pm daily (at certain times of the day visitors may need to wait for prayers to finish)

Camera ₹300

■ Female visitors should be accompanied by a man, but this rule is not followed strictly.

■ Dress respectfully – no shorts, short skirts or sleeveless tops. It is a good idea to come with appropriate clothing, although overgarments are provided if needed.

■ You cannot eat or drink within the mosque itself, but Karim's (*see p89*) is close by, and there are many roadside cafés.

### ⑩ The Domes
Three huge onion domes sit atop the main prayer hall, their bulbous outlines picked out in delicate black stripes. The central dome is partially obscured by the massive *iwan* in front, an architectural conundrum that even Shah Jahan's master architects were unable to resolve.

# TOP 10 ⭐ Humayun's Tomb

Built in the 1560s, this gigantic mausoleum is the first of the great Mughal garden tombs and the final resting place of the ill-fated emperor Humayun (r 1530–40 and 1555–6). The mausoleum is one of Delhi's most impressive sights and a classic example of the tradition of tomb-building which, almost 100 years later, was to reach its zenith in the Taj Mahal. It is also one of the most peaceful places in Delhi, with a huge expanse of beautiful gardens and an absorbing cluster of tombs, gateways and mosques.

### 1 The Western Gateway

The entrance to the gardens is through the western gateway **(left)**. This serves as a kind of architectural curtain, designed to conceal the garden and tomb from the visitor's view until the very last minute, when Humayun's magnificent mausoleum appears in all its glory.

**Humayun's Tomb map**

### 2 Mosque and Tomb of Isa Khan

The florid octagonal mosque and tomb of Isa Khan **(below)**, a courtier during the reign of Sher Shah Suri (r 1540–45), provides a complete change of style. Both mosque and tomb lie within their own garden, enclosed in fortress-like walls.

### 3 The Gardens

The beautiful gardens that surround the tomb follow the Persian-style *charbagh* pattern, in which the garden is divided into four quarters by water channels: a representation of the Islamic gardens of paradise.

### 4 The Barber's Tomb

According to legend, this elegant tomb was built for the imperial barber – a rather fitting memorial to the person who was trusted to hold a razor to the emperor's throat.

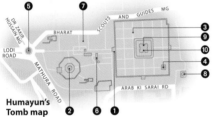

**5 Sabz Burj**
Housing the grave of an unknown Mughal nobleman, this beautiful blue-domed, Persian-style tomb now stands marooned on a busy roundabout near the entrance to the complex.

**8 Nila Gumbad**
The striking Persian-style Nila Gumbad, with its blue-tiled dome, houses the remains of an unknown Mughal nobleman.

**9 The Tomb**
Set atop a raised platform, the mausoleum **(below)** is topped by a massive dome. Each of its four façades is dominated by a huge arch.

### HUMAYUN

The second Mughal emperor, Humayun, was an endearingly irresolute figure, who alternated between bouts of utter military brilliance and total self-indulgence. After succeeding his father Babur in 1530, he lost his empire to the Afghan invader Sher Shah Suri, and was obliged to seek refuge in Persia for the next 15 years – until he won the empire back. His luck didn't last: one year later he was dead, having fallen down a very steep flight of steps in the Purana Qila (see p93).

**6 The Arab Serai**
This extensive walled garden is where visiting crafters are thought to have lived while they worked on the tomb. It also houses the neat little Afsarwala Mosque and Tomb.

**7 Bu Halima's Garden**
The entrance to the complex is through Bu Halima's garden, which has its own gateway. This gateway pre-dates the tomb itself, although the mausoleum and the garden were designed in alignment to it.

**10 The Interior**
A single door on the southern side opens into the mausoleum's interior **(right)**, where Humayun lies in a small, plain marble tomb.

### NEED TO KNOW

**MAP S6** ▪ Off Mathura Road ▪ Taxi, auto-rickshaw or JLN Stadium Metro

**Open** Sunrise–sunset daily

Adm ₹600, card/online ₹550 (Indians ₹40, ₹35 card/online), video ₹25

▪ Walking clockwise around the exterior of the tomb before going inside gives a sense of the scale of the mausoleum. The walk also takes in the Barber's Tomb and Nila Gumbad, after which the tomb can be entered via the southern entrance.

▪ There is also a small museum set inside the Western Gateway.

# TOP 10 ⭐ Around Kartavya Path

Running east to west through the heart of New Delhi, Kartavya Path (formerly Rajpath) is the grandest of all the city's boulevards, stretching 2 km (1 mile) from India Gate to the presidential palace, Rashtrapati Bhavan. Called Kingsway by the British, it was created to showcase spectacular processions and occasions of state, while the surrounding central government buildings were intended to serve as an enduring symbol of British pomp and power.

### 3 Cathedral Church of the Redemption

Designed by Henry Medd, this 1935 Neo-Classical church **(left)** was largely inspired by Andrea Palladio's Il Redentore in Venice, and is one of the biggest and most impressive churches in Delhi.

### 4 Raisina Hill

The area of Raisina Hill rises between the Secretariat Buildings towards Rashtrapati Bhavan, although the latter only becomes visible once you reach the top, a miscalculation that infuriated Lutyens.

### 1 Secretariat Buildings

Flanking Raisina Hill are the Secretariat Buildings. Designed by Herbert Baker in Neo-Classical style with Indian touches.

### 5 Kartavya Path

This grand 2-km (1-mile) axis connects India Gate with Rashtrapati Bhavan, linking many of New Delhi's major buildings along the way.

### 2 Rashtrapati Bhavan

Once the viceroy's residence and now home to the President of India, the magnificent Rashtrapati Bhavan **(below)** is Edwin Lutyens' masterpiece, a unique fusion of European and Indian elements. Visitors can register in advance for a guided tour.

### 6 Sansad Bhavan

Built for the Legislative Assembly in 1935, this circular building to the north of Kartavya Path was home to the Indian parliament after independence. The triangular structure next to it is the new parliament building completed as part of the Central Vista Project.

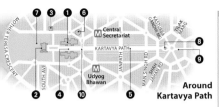

Around
Kartavya Path

### 7 Amrit Udyan
Set in the grounds of Rashtrapati Bhavan, this Mughal-style garden is laid out with watercourses, fountains and neat squares of manicured lawn.

### 8 India Gate
This imposing arch commemorates the soldiers killed in World War I and the Afghan Wars. Below the arch, the Tomb of the Unknown Soldier **(above)** honours those who died during the 1971 Indo-Pakistan conflict.

### 9 National War Memorial
Just beyond India Gate is the National War Memorial **(left)**. The layout of the memorial features four large concentric circles, with an obelisk at the centre. It also houses the Amar Jawan Jyoti, an eternal flame that symbolizes the immortality of the spirit of fallen soldiers.

**EDWIN LUTYENS**

Edwin Landseer Lutyens (1869–1944) was the master architect behind New Delhi and worked on the new city for over 20 years. During that time Lutyens developed an Indian-influenced Neo-Classical style, best seen in the grand Rashtrapati Bhavan, with its enormous Buddhist-inspired dome. The success of Lutyens' designs is slightly surprising, especially given his self-confessed dislike of Indian architecture.

### 10 Vijay Chowk
Formerly known as the Grand Place, Vijay Chowk is an enormous crossroads marking the point at which Kartavya Path meets Raisina Hill.

**NEED TO KNOW**

**MAP L3** ■ Central Secretariat Metro & Udyog Bhawan Metro

*Rashtrapati Bhavan:* 2301 5321 (tours); www.rashtrapatisachivalaya.gov.in/rbtour

■ The ongoing Central Vista Project is a redevelopment of the nation's power corridor, the 2-km- (1-mile-) long Rajpath, now renamed Kartavya Path. It envisages a new parliament building, a common central Secretariat, an office and residence of the prime minister and a vice-president enclave. Some parts of the project are not yet complete so please check (https://centralvista.gov.in/#slide-6) before visiting the sites around Kartavya Path.

*Following pages Jama Masjid in Old Delhi*

# TOP 10 ⭐ Qutb Minar Complex

Towering over southern Delhi, the monumental Qutb Minar is one of the city's most dramatic and instantly recognizable landmarks: a triumphal minaret that marked, with a flourish, both the coming of Islam to the subcontinent and the arrival of the Delhi sultans, who held power in northern India for around 400 years. Further remarkable monuments, including India's oldest mosque, lie scattered at the foot of the minaret and nearby, around Mehrauli village.

### ② Iron Pillar

This unusual pillar **(left)**, in the central courtyard, is thought to have been made in Bihar in the 4th century and later brought to Delhi by the Tomars. Remarkably, it has remained rust free for over 1,500 years.

### ③ Tomb of Imam Zamin

The tomb houses the remains of the Turkestani religious itinerant Imam Zamin (d 1539) and postdates the Qutb Minar complex.

### ① Quwwat-ul-Islam

The first mosque in Delhi, the Quwwat-ul-Islam (Might of Islam), was built by Qutbuddin Aibak (r 1206–10) in 1192, soon after Muhammad Ghori's conquest *(see p42)* of northwest India.

### ④ Qutb Minar

Built during the reigns of Aibak and Iltutmish (r 1211–36), this tapering minaret **(right)** is 72 m (236 ft) tall. A fifth storey, clad in marble, was added later, after the summit was damaged by lightning.

### 8 Madrasa of Alauddin Khilji

Built around 1317 as a *madrasa* (religious school), this plain building **(left)** has lost most of its original stone facing. Alauddin (r 1296–1316) himself is thought to be buried in its central chamber.

### 9 Alai Minar

A large stump of rough stone is all that remains of a rather maverick scheme to build a second oversized minaret, intended to be even greater than the mighty Qutb Minar.

### 5 Tomb of Iltutmish

Immediately behind the mosque is the tomb of Iltutmish, one of the principal architects of the Qutb Minar complex. Small and plain on the outside, the tomb is lavishly carved within.

### 6 Alai Darwaza

Built in 1311 as a brand new gateway to the mosque, the Alai Darwaza is richly carved using red sandstone and white marble, a hallmark of the later Mughal style.

Qutb Minar Complex map

### 10 The Prayer Hall Screen

One of the finest pieces of Islamic architecture in all of India, the Quwwat-ul-Islam's prayer hall screen **(left)** is composed of five sharply pointed arches that are covered in Koranic inscriptions and floral decoration.

### 7 The Central Courtyard

Aibak demolished 27 Hindu and Jain temples to make way for his mosque. The temple pillars were incorporated into the arcade of the central courtyard **(below)**, giving it a Hindu appearance.

---

**THE TOWER OF BABEL, DELHI STYLE**

The Alai Minar was the brainchild of Alauddin Khilji, the most brilliant and ruthless of all the Delhi sultans. The plan was to build a minaret twice the height of the Qutb Minar, but the gargantuan project never really got off the ground, and all that remains is a large pile of rubble – "a frustrated tower of Babel", as one writer describes it.

---

**NEED TO KNOW**

**MAP U3** ■ Mehrauli, Delhi-Gurugram Road ■ Taxi, auto-rickshaw or Qutab Minar Metro

**Open** Sunrise–sunset daily

Adm ₹600, card/online ₹550 (Indians ₹40, card/online ₹35), video ₹50, audio guide ₹100 plus tax and a deposit of ID, credit card or ₹2,000

...................................................

■ Arrive early or late to avoid the coach parties.

■ There are drink stalls around the entrance to the complex. For food, it is best to bring a picnic.

# Sites around Mehrauli

The beautiful and intricately designed Rajon ki Bain stepwell

### 1 Rajon ki Bain
Built in 1506, this superb *baoli* (stepwell) is atmospherically buried amid woodland in the heart of the park. It has been built up over four levels, with rooms and arcades around the top two floors and a well situated at the bottom.

### 2 Jamali-Kamali Masjid and Tomb
This beautiful early Mughal mosque, built by the poet Sheikh Fazlullah (known as Jamali; d. 1535), has a delicately carved façade and characteristic red sandstone and white marble stonework. The poet's tomb is located in an enclosure beside the mosque.

Ceiling detail, Jamali-Kamali Tomb

### 3 Adham Khan's Tomb
Mughal emperor Akbar built this tomb for his foster brother, who was thrown to his death from Agra Fort's battlements for murdering one of Akbar's generals. The tomb's labyrinthine interior has earned it the nickname *bhulbhulaiyan* (maze).

### 4 Quli Khan's Tomb
Erected for Adham Khan's brother, Mohammad Quli Khan, this neat little tomb was converted into a summer retreat by Sir Thomas Metcalfe. It was christened Dilkusha, or "Heart's Delight"; the ruined walls can still be seen around the tomb.

### 5 Balban's Tomb
Close to the Jamali-Kamali Masjid lie the fragments of the tomb of Balban (1200–87), one of the most powerful of the early Delhi sultans.

### 6 Madhi Masjid
Constructed in the early Mughal era, this heavily fortified building looks more like a fortress than a mosque, with a large courtyard and – unusually – two separate prayer halls on either side of a central *mihrab* wall.

### 7 Dargah Qutb Sahib
In the heart of the Mehrauli bazaar (ask locally for directions), this serene little religious complex

honours Qutbuddin Bakhtiyar Kaki (d 1235), a Sufi saint from Fergana (in modern Uzbekistan).

### 8 Zafar Mahal

This summer palace complex is the last structure the Mughals built. It was started by Akbar Shah II (1760–1837) and was completed by his son, Bahadur Shah Zafar, the last Mughal emperor.

**A courtyard within the Jahaz Mahal**

### 9 Jahaz Mahal

At the western end of Mehrauli village, this enigmatic Lodi-era structure is thought to have been either a travellers' rest house or an opulent royal pleasure palace.

### 10 Mehrauli Archaeological Park

West of the Qutb, this park was set up to protect the ancient monuments dotted around the area, including over 70, dating from the 11th to the 19th centuries, in the park itself.

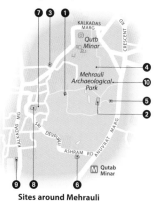

**Sites around Mehrauli**

## METCALFE'S FOLLY

Mehrauli witnessed one of the stranger episodes in Anglo-Indian history when Sir Thomas Theophilus Metcalfe (1795–1853), British Resident at the Mughal Court, decided to establish a summer residence in the area. Rather than build a new house, Metcalfe made the unusual decision to convert the tomb of Quli Khan into an English-style country residence. He christened this new building Dilkusha (Heart's Delight), although it is generally known as Metcalfe's Folly. The tomb's central chamber was turned into a dining room. Alongside the main structure, a pair of flanking wings and various outbuildings were erected (remnants of which can still be seen). As fate would have it, Metcalfe's love of all things Mughal did him little good: he died slowly, allegedly poisoned by one of the emperor's queens.

**The tomb of Quli Khan**

# TOP 10 ★ National Crafts Museum

This enjoyable museum showcases India's incredible variety of local artistic and cultural traditions in a rustic building and walled garden designed by Charles Correa (1930–2015). There are some fascinating crafts here from every part of the subcontinent and in every medium, from traditional costumes to ivory carvings. There is even a complete miniature village of traditional buildings from across India in the grounds outside.

### 3 Folk and Tribal Art

This gallery **(left)** is packed with unusual objects dating from the 19th century to the present day, from a collection of traditional dolls to religious items.

### 4 Outdoor Exhibits

The museum's grounds are dotted with a number of exhibits, such as stone carvings from Rajasthan and Indo-Chinese statues from Tamil Nadu.

### 5 Cultic Objects Gallery

This gallery houses religious objects from across India, ranging from Hindu bronzes and south Indian paintings to unique Jain and Tibetan Buddhist artifacts.

### 6 Bhuta Sculpture Gallery

Devoted to the Bhuta cult of Karnataka, this gallery **(left)** contains images from the shrine of Nandikeshvara in Udipi province, carved in dark jackfruit wood and featuring striking human and animal-headed figures.

---

**NEED TO KNOW**

**MAP R3** ■ Bhairon Marg ■ 233 71370 ■ Pragati Maidan Metro

**Open** 10am–5pm Tue–Sun

Adm ₹200 (Indians ₹20), camera ₹500

■ The museum is good for crafts shopping, but do research beforehand. It is best to visit the government emporiums around Connaught Place to see what is available and get an idea of prices.

■ Permission to take photographs can be obtained from reception.

■ Visit Café Lota *(78389 60787)*, inside the museum, known for its fusion Indian cuisine, teas and coffees.

### 1 Museum Building

Designed by Indian architect Charles Correa, this rustic, ochre-coloured building, encircled by shady verandahs and set in a tree-filled compound, feels like a rural village in the heart of Delhi.

### 2 Resident Craftspeople

The small courtyard, at the back of the museum, is home to a selection of stalls. Artisans can often be seen at work on a wide range of crafts, such as painting, stone carving, metalworking and weaving. They also sell their products.

### 8 Traditional Buildings

Scattered around the museum garden is a fascinating collection of traditional buildings from across India, including a a traditional house **(left)** from Kullu in the state of Himachal Pradesh.

### GALLERY GUIDE

The National Crafts Museum is relatively small and can be covered in a couple of hours. All the galleries are laid out over the ground floor of the building, except the Textile Gallery and a section of the Court Crafts Gallery, which are tucked away upstairs.

**7** Textile Gallery

**Key to Floorplan**
  Ground floor
  First floor

**10** Court Crafts Gallery

**10** Court Crafts Gallery

**5** Cultic Objects Gallery

**2** Resident Craftspeople

**3** Folk and Tribal Art

**8** Traditional Buildings

**9** Shopping for Crafts

**1** The Museum Building

**6** Bhuta Sculpture Gallery

**National Crafts Museum floorplan**

### 7 Textile Gallery

This beautiful, well-curated gallery provides an overview of India's textile traditions, with a vast collection of fabrics in styles including brocade, block printing, tie-dye and appliqué.

### 9 Shopping for Crafts

The museum has one of Delhi's most interesting selections of traditional crafts for sale, either from one of the stalls at the back of the museum **(below)**, or the shop.

### 10 Court Crafts Gallery

Aristocratic arts from the 18th century to today are displayed here, including *bidri*-ware (silver inlay work) **(above)**, enamel-ware, jade, ivory carvings and glass jewellery.

# TOP 10 ⭐ Lodi Gardens

One of the most enjoyable excursions in Delhi, the beautiful Lodi Gardens offer a winning combination of nature and history. The gardens themselves are among the most attractive and relaxed in the city, with quiet paths winding between tropical trees and plentiful birdlife in the branches overhead. The series of fine medieval tombs dotted among the trees and lawns, erected by nobles of the Lodi and Sayyid Dynasties during the later years of the Delhi Sultanate, provide historical interest.

## ② Muhammad Shah's Tomb

The tomb **(left)** of Sayyid ruler Muhammad Shah (r 1434–44) is built in the octagonal shape favoured by the later Delhi sultans. Its main dome is surrounded by eight small *chhatris*.

## ③ The Gardens

The gardens were created in 1936 by Lady Willingdon, wife of the viceroy and governor-general of India. She had the two villages that stood here demolished to make way for the new gardens.

## ① Sikander Lodi's Tomb

At the northern end of the gardens is the tomb of Sikander Lodi (r 1489–1517), the penultimate Delhi sultan. It occupies an idyllic garden and has interior walls that feature the remains of the original blue tilework.

### THE SAYYID AND LODI DYNASTIES

The Sayyid and Lodi Dynasties held sway from 1414 until 1526, though their power was challenged by a series of internal rebellions and external threats. The first Sayyid sultan, Khizr Khan, rose to power after Timur's invasion in 1398; while the last sultan, Ibrahim Lodi (r 1517–26), was killed by Timur's great-great-great-grandson, Babur, who was the founder of the Mughal Dynasty.

## ④ National Bonsai Garden

Near the southern entrance to the park, the National Bonsai Garden has a collection of tiny trees. A few displays show the various styles of traditional bonsai.

## ⑤ Athpula

Located near the tomb of Sikander Lodi, the striking, graceful Athpula (Eight Piers) bridge **(above)** was built during the reign of Mughal emperor Akbar (r 1556–1605).

### 6 Shish Gumbad
Built around 1600 for an unidentified nobleman, this is a cuboid-shaped tomb **(below)**, enlivened with bands of rich blue tiles, which run around the middle and top.

### 8 Bara Gumbad Masjid
Attached to the Bara Gumbad Tomb, this mosque is small but lavishly decorated, with swirls of Koranic script **(right)** covering every available surface.

**Lodi Gardens map**

### 9 Round Tower
To the east of the Bara Gumbad stands a solid-looking round tower, probably built during the 14th century.

### 10 Bara Gumbad Tomb
Dating from around 1500, the Bara Gumbad Tomb is the gardens' most impressive structure, a cuboid tomb (occupant unknown), topped by a massive dome. Its rather severe outlines are relieved by alternating panels of red and black stone.

### 7 Birdlife
The gardens are home to a rich array of birdlife, including tree pies, Indian rollers, spotted owlets, geese and green parakeets **(right)**.

**NEED TO KNOW**

**MAP N6** ■ Lodi Road
■ Taxi, auto-rickshaw or Jor Bagh Metro

**Open** Apr–Sep: 5am–8pm daily (Oct–Mar: from 6am daily)

*National Bonsai Garden:* open 9am–5pm Mon–Sat; closed public hols

■ There is nowhere to eat or drink within the gardens, but you are welcome to bring a picnic with you.

■ The India Habitat Centre, near the southern entrance on Lodi Road, has a couple of attractive cafés.

# TOP 10 ⭐ National Museum

Founded in 1949, the superb National Museum is India's finest, with a collection of over 200,000 exhibits charting five millennia of subcontinental history. Every major strand in India's complex cultural identity is covered here, with artifacts from across the country and beyond, including prehistoric archaeological finds, Buddhist statues, Chola bronzes and Mughal miniatures.

**1 Mughal Emperor Shah Jahan in Dara Shikoh's Marriage Procession**

Painted around 1750 in Awadh, this painting **(below)** is a good example of superbly detailed Indian miniature art, portraying the wedding procession of Shah Jahan's favourite son, Dara Shikoh.

**4 Dancing Girl**

This small but famous image of an elegant, long-legged dancing girl **(left)** was found in Mohenjodaro. Dating from around 2500 BCE, it is one of the world's oldest cast-bronze statuettes.

**2 Harappan Bronze Chariot**

One of the museum's most charming pieces is a bronze figurine (c 2000 BCE) of a man on a chariot pulled by oxen.

**3 Avalokitesvara**

These rare 9th- and 10th-century silk paintings, from the town of Dunhuang on the old Silk Route in northwestern China, depict Avalokitesvara, the Bodhisattva of Infinite Compassion, a deity of Vajrayana Buddhism.

**5 Ganga**

This 5th-century Gupta terracotta statue **(below)** is one of the museum's most graceful. The river goddess Ganga is seen walking on the back of her mythical animal mount, the crocodile-like *makara*, whilst carrying an urn.

**NEED TO KNOW**

**MAP N3** ■ 11 Janpath, south of Kartavya Path ■ 2301 9272 ■ Udyog Bhawan Metro ■ www. nationalmuseum india.gov.in

**Open** 10am–6pm Tue–Sun; closed Mon & public hols

Adm ₹650 (Indians ₹20), including audio guide.

■ The museum regularly closes areas or galleries for renovation. It is best to call ahead or check the website first.

■ The collection on display is huge, so take your time and don't try to

see everything at once. The audio guides available here pick out around 30 of the best exhibits.

■ There is a small café on the museum premises, which sells snacks and refreshments.

**GALLERY GUIDE**

The museum's wide-ranging collection is arranged over three floors, although almost all of the best exhibits are to be found on the ground floor of the building. The first nine exhibits described here are displayed on the ground floor, while the tenth is on the first floor. The reception area has books and replicas of some of the exhibits for sale. A visit to the extensive library can be valuable for researchers.

### ⑦ Shiva Nataraja

This iconic 12th-century Chola bronze **(left)** shows Shiva as *nataraj* ("lord of dance"), surrounded by a ring of fire, representing the cycle of life. He is performing *tandava*, the cosmic dance of destruction and creation.

### ⑥ Mughal Nativity Painting

This Muslim version of a usually Christian subject **(below)** may seem surprising, but Jesus is revered as a prophet by Muslims, and Mary is mentioned more in the Koran than in the Bible.

### ⑧ Baluchari Sari

Rare 18th-century silk saris with delicate floral patterns are part of the collection. They were made in Murshidabad (West Bengal), one of the country's most famous silk production centres.

### ⑩ Kali

The fearsome goddess Kali, one of the more favoured deities of the Cholas, appears serenely poised and unusually benign in an outstanding late 12th-century bronze.

### ⑨ Asita's Visit to Suddhadhana

This is a beautifully carved stone bas-relief **(right)** from the great Satavahana-era Buddhist monastery of Amaravati (Andhra Pradesh), dating from the 1st–2nd century CE. The panel depicts the sage Asita visiting King Suddhadhana in the town of Lumbini to admire his son, the newly born Buddha.

# National Museum Collections

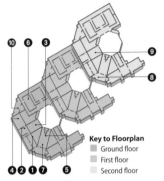

**Key to Floorplan**
- Ground floor
- First floor
- Second floor

**National Museum Collections**

## 1 Kushan (Gandhara, Mathura and Ikshavaku Art)

This superb collection of classical sculpture from the Gandhara kingdom (in Afghanistan) is famous for its remarkable Indo-Greek culture, in which local Buddhist traditions intermingled with the Greek styles brought to the region by Alexander the Great (356–23 BCE).

## 2 Gupta Terracotta and Early Medieval Art

The classic art of the Guptas (3rd–5th centuries), the second of India's great dynasties, is on show here, alongside some of the more flamboyant statues from the early Pallava (300–900 CE) and Chola (300 BCE–1279 CE) kingdoms of the south, featuring beautiful, intricately carved Hindu gods.

## 3 Bronzes

This is one of the museum's highlights: a room full of Chola bronze statues of Hindu deities, including one of the most iconic images of Indian art – a pair of Shiva *natarajas*.

## 4 Late Medieval Art

Outstanding examples of the sculptural arts that flourished across central and southern India during the 11th and 12th centuries feature in this excellent collection, including those from the Vijayanagar, Hoysala, Chola and Pala kingdoms.

## 5 Harappan Civilization

The museum is one of the world's finest showcases of artifacts from the Indus Valley Civilization (c 2500–1500 BCE). On display are a wide range of finds from Harappa, Mohenjodaro and elsewhere, vividly bringing one of the world's most ancient cultures to life.

## 6 Indian Miniature Paintings

Another of the museum's highlights, this is an extensive collection of superbly detailed and vibrant paintings from the schools of Rajasthani, Pahari, Deccani and Mughal.

## 7 Maurya, Sunga and Satavahana Art

These galleries are devoted to the art of the Mauryans (321–185 BCE), India's first great empire, and their successors. Displays include monumental sculptures, bas-relief carvings and stone pillars, most recovered

**Sunga sculpture of an amorous couple**

## INDIAN MINIATURE PAINTING

Although originally of Persian origin, the art of the miniature was perfected in India, where artists developed a distinctive style of brilliantly coloured and minutely detailed painting, usually depicting either religious subjects or scenes from courtly life. Miniature painting flourished under Muslim patronage throughout India – the Mughals, in particular, commissioned thousands of pictures and illustrated manuscripts, while distinctive regional schools subsequently developed in Rajasthan, the Deccan and across the Pahari region in the Himalayan foothills. Most artists remain anonymous, although a few of the most famous are listed on the right.

**TOP 10
MINIATURE PAINTERS**

**1** Mir Sayyid Ali (Persian/ Mughal, 16th century)

**2** Abd al-Samad (Persian/ Mughal, 16th century)

**3** Basawan (Mughal, 16th century)

**4** Mansur (Mughal, 17th century)

**5** Bishandas (Mughal, 17th century)

**6** Abu al-Hasan (Mughal, 17th century)

**7** Govardhan (Mughal, 17th century)

**8** Bichitr (Mughal, 17th century)

**9** Sahibdin (Rajasthan, 17th century)

**10** Dalchand (Rajasthan, 18th century)

**Miniature painting (1725–30)** from Bundi, Rajasthan, depicting ladies playing *chaupar*, National Museum

from Buddhist temples, including panels from the Buddhist monastery of Amaravati in Andhra Pradesh *(see p33)*.

### 8 Decorative Arts and Textiles

Dedicated to India's rich and varied clothing and textile traditions, this gallery features a colourful display of woven, printed, tie-dyed, embroidered and appliqué-worked fabrics in silk, cotton and wool. Examples of India's varied decorative arts, including exquisite artifacts made from ivory, jade, glass, ceramic and wood, fill the adjoining galleries.

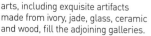

**Silver-incised bowl, Decorative Arts Gallery**

### 9 Tribal Lifestyle

This is a rare glimpse into the lives of India's northeastern tribes. Exhibits include simple weapons, household items and some unusual headgear, backed up by fascinating black-and-white photos of tribe members in traditional attire.

### 10 Buddhist Art

A wide range of Buddhist art and artifacts from across India, Nepal, Gandhara and China are on display here, including some rare *thangkas* (devotional paintings), statues and a pair of fine silver-and-brass temple trumpets from Ladakh.

# 🔟 ⭐ Taj Mahal, Agra and Fatehpur Sikri

In 1504, Sikandar Lodi moved his capital from Delhi to Agra. Shah Jahan moved it back in 1638, but when his favourite wife – Mumtaz (or "Taj") Mahal – died before the move, the grief-stricken emperor had this magnificent tomb built for her in Agra. Of unparalleled beauty, the Taj is the zenith of Mughal architecture. Agra has other wonderful Mughal structures, and just down the road, Shah Jahan's grandfather, Akbar, had an entire city built at Fatehpur Sikri.

**4 The Tomb**
The Taj Mahal's classic perfection is rooted in the simplest of architectural concepts. The main tomb is a perfect cube, while the dome itself is of equal height to the building on which it rests.

**1 The Charbagh**
The Taj sits at the far end of one of the finest Mughal *charbagh*-style gardens **(above)**, an expanse of lawn divided into four by raised marble water channels.

**5 The Dome**
The dome rises to a height of 73 m (240 ft), topped by a lotus-shaped design and surrounded by four smaller *chhatris* (domed pavilions), echoing those that cap the four minarets.

**2 Chowk-i-Jilo Khana**
The Chowk-i-Jilo Khana is a forecourt. At its northern edge is a gateway, which leads to the Taj but screens it from the view of those outside.

**6 Minarets**
Minarets mark each of the four corners. Unusually, these are detached from the main tomb, so that if any of them ever fell, they would collapse away from the principal structure.

**3 Tomb Chamber**
The tomb of Mumtaz Mahal **(below)** sits at the centre of the atmospheric tomb chamber, and is protected by an exquisitely detailed *jali* (carved screen), while the tomb of Shah Jahan lies alongside it.

**7 The Lotus Pool**
The centre of the *charbagh's* four intersecting water channels is marked by the marble Lotus Pool, symbolizing the pool in the Islamic gardens of paradise.

**8 Calligraphic Panels**
Koranic inscriptions frame the tomb's four archways. The script in the higher panels has been enlarged to compensate for the distorting effects of perspective.

## ⑨ Mosque and Mehman Khana

The Taj is flanked by two mirror-image buildings: a mosque **(above)** and the Mehman Khana, or *jawab* (response). The *jawab* cannot be used for worship since it is oriented the wrong way round.

Taj Mahal, a masterpiece of unparalleled beauty

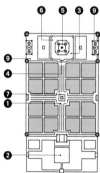

Taj Mahal plan

### NEED TO KNOW

**MAP C3**

*Taj Mahal:* Taj Ganj, Agra, 215 km (134 miles) SE of Delhi; open 30 min before sunrise–30 min before sunset Sat–Thu; adm ₹1050 plus ₹200 for the main mausoleum www.tajmahal.gov.in

*Fatehpur Sikri:* 45 km (28 miles) SW of Agra; open sunrise–sunset daily; adm ₹550 (Indians ₹40), video ₹25 (the Jama Masjid and the museum are free to enter)

■ Arrive early at the Taj to avoid the crowds. Security is tight and visitors cannot bring in food, drink (apart from a bottle of water), phones or even guidebooks. There are a number of cafés outside in Taj Ganj.

■ There are small archaeological museums that can be visited at both sites *(open 9am–5pm Sat–Thu)*.

## ⑩ Pietra Dura

Large parts of the Taj Mahal's exterior walls are covered in excellent *pietra dura* inlay **(above)**, in which intricate stylized geometrical floral patterns are created using coloured precious and semiprecious stones.

# Sights in Agra

**① Sikandra**
MAP C3 ■ Open sunrise–
sunset daily ■ Adm
One of the grandest of all the
Mughal monuments, this perfectly
symmetrical complex is home to
Akbar's impressive red sandstone
mausoleum. His tomb is located in
the centre of a vast, walled garden.

**The tomb of Akbar, Sikandra**

**② Taj Nature Walk**
MAP C3 ■ Open summer:
7am–7pm daily; winter: 8am–5pm
daily ■ Adm ■ www.tajmahal.gov.in
A 9-km- (5.5-mile-) long nature trail
with lovely views of the Taj.

**③ Mehtab Bagh**
MAP C3 ■ Open sunrise–
sunset daily ■ Adm
The Moonlight Garden offers the
ultimate view of the Taj Mahal.

**④ Itimad-ud-Daulah**
MAP C3 ■ Open sunrise–
sunset daily ■ Adm
Built by Nur Jahan (1577–1645), this
tomb is decorated with *pietra dura*.

**Itimad-ud-Daulah**

**⑤ Agra Fort**
MAP C3 ■ Open sunrise–sunset
daily ■ Adm and charge for video
The Agra Fort was originally built by
Akbar (1542–1605) and enlarged and
embellished by Jahangir (1569–1627)
and Shah Jahan (1592–1666).

**⑥ Jama Masjid**
MAP C3 ■ Open sunrise–
sunset daily
Built in 1648, this spectacular
mosque is a perfect example of
the late-Mughal architectural style
perfected during the reign of
Shah Jahan.

**⑦ Kinari Bazaar**
MAP C3 ■ Open 11:30am–
6pm Mon–Sat
This atmospheric bazaar is known
for its fine jewellery and for the best
*petha*, an unusual confection made
from crystallized pumpkin.

**⑧ Chini-ka-Rauza**
MAP C3 ■ Open daily
This Persian-style tomb (1628-39)
was built for Afzal Khan, a poet who
served as Shah Jahan's minister.

**⑨ Rambagh Gardens**
MAP C3 ■ Open sunrise–
sunset daily ■ Adm
These formal gardens are laid out in
the traditional Persian *charbagh* plan.

**⑩ Mariam's Tomb**
MAP C3 ■ Open sunrise–
sunset daily ■ Adm
This pretty tomb was built in honour
of Mariam Zamani, one of Akbar's
wives and mother of Jahangir.

# Sights in Fatehpur Sikri

**The impressive Jama Masjid on a sunny day**

**1 Jama Masjid**
The magnificent Jama Masjid, one of the biggest mosques in India, houses the tomb of the Sufi saint Salim Chisti. It is entered through a massive, spectacular gate called the Buland Darwaza, which leads into the mosque's huge courtyard.

**2 Diwan-i-Aam**
It was in this courtyard that the emperor received subjects. The surrounding colonnade is topped with Hindu-style capitals.

**3 Diwan-i-Khas**
The emperor's private audience hall deliberately combines Muslim, Hindu, Buddhist and Christian features.

**4 Hiran Minar**
Just outside the city to the north, the odd-looking Hiran Minar is a beacon tower said to be built over the grave of Akbar's favourite elephant.

**Hiran Minar**

**5 Pachisi Court**
In the palace's main courtyard there is a giant outdoor board for *pachisi*, the original version of ludo. It is believed that Akbar would play a life-size version of the game with colourfully dressed courtesans forming the live pieces.

**6 House of the Turkish Sultana**
This small stone building is known for its intricate wood-like carvings and the latticework on the screens. Too small for a residence, it was more likely used as a pleasure pavilion attached to the pond.

**7 Daulat Khana**
Akbar's private quarters have three parts. The library once housed his collection of over 25,000 manuscripts. The room behind it was his study, and upstairs was his bedroom, known as the *khwabgah*.

**8 Panch Mahal**
The "five-storey palace" narrows with each successive floor and marks the beginning of the *zenana* or women's quarters. Its columns originally had screens between them, shielding the women from view.

**9 Sunehra Makan**
Akbar's mother may have lived in the "golden house". Its interior murals, although sadly faded, are still impressive.

**10 Jodhabai's Palace**
The main harem was home to Akbar's senior wives (he had 13 wives in all). It is a grand affair, modelled on the ornate palaces of the Hindu Rajputs.

# The Top 10
# of Everything

**Praying at the shrine
in Nizamuddin**

| | |
|---|---|
| Moments in History | 42 |
| Delhi Sultanate Sights | 44 |
| Mughal Delhi Sights | 46 |
| Monuments of the 1857 Uprising | 48 |
| Cities of Delhi, Old and New | 50 |
| Places of Worship | 52 |
| Museums and Galleries | 54 |
| Delhi-Inspired Books | 56 |
| Parks and Gardens | 58 |
| Off the Beaten Track | 60 |
| Performing Arts Venues | 62 |
| Places to Eat | 64 |
| Bazaars of Old Delhi | 66 |
| Delhi for Free | 68 |
| Festivals and Events | 70 |
| Excursions from Delhi | 72 |

#  Moments in History

**The citadel of Qila Rai Pithora**

### 1 736 CE: Founding of Delhi

Delhi was founded by the Rajput Tomars in the Surajkund area, south of the modern city. In 1060, the town was relocated 10 km (6 miles) west by Tomar ruler Anangpal II, who created a new fortified citadel there called Lal Kot. Around 1160, the Tomars became vassals of the Chauhans, another Rajput clan from Ajmer, who extended Lal Kot and renamed it Qila Rai Pithora.

### 2 1192: Founding of the Delhi Sultanate

Muhammad of Ghor, from Ghazni (Afghanistan), invaded north India in 1191, but was defeated by Prithviraj Chauhan III at the Battle of Tarain. A year later, Muhammad returned, defeated Prithviraj and took control of northern India. He went home, leaving Qutbuddin Aibak, his general, in charge of Delhi. Aibak became the first sultan of Delhi following Muhammad Ghori's death in 1206.

### 3 1327 and 1398: Decline of the Delhi Sultanate

In 1327, Muhammad bin Tughlaq moved the capital from Delhi to Daulatabad (present-day Devagiri in Maharashtra). However, Tughlaq's administrative failures marked the beginning of the Delhi Sultanate's decline. The Sultante's fall followed soon after Timur (Tamerlaine) sacked Delhi in 1398 and left it in ruins.

### 4 1526: Arrival of the First Mughals

Babur, a Central Asian adventurer and former ruler of Fergana, Kabul and Samarkand, defeated the last Delhi sultan, Ibrahim Lodi, at the Battle of Panipat (1526) and ushered in the Mughal Dynasty.

### 5 1638: Foundation of Shajahanabad

The fifth Mughal emperor, Shah Jahan, transferred India's capital from Agra (where it had been moved by his predecessor, Akbar) back to Delhi. Once there, he founded the new city of Shahjahanabad, or Old Delhi, as it is known today.

### 6 1857: Indian Uprising

In 1857, Indian soldiers across north India revolted and seized control of major cities under company rule, including Delhi, Lucknow and Kanpur. Delhi became the focus of the movement, as the sepoys rallied behind the Mughal emperor, Bahadur Shah Zafar II. The rebellion was quelled after months of bitter fighting but as a consequence, the British Crown took direct control over the subcontinent – establishing "The Raj".

**A depiction of the 1857 Uprising**

## 7 1911: Foundation of New Delhi

The capital of British India was moved from Calcutta to Delhi and work began on building the grandiose city of New Delhi under the creative leadership of Edwin Lutyens. The city was inaugurated in 1931 – ironically, the same year the British agreed, in principle, to grant India its independence at a future date.

**Celebrating Indian independence**

## 8 1947: Independence

India was partitioned and became independent. Delhi lost a large proportion of its former Muslim population, while huge numbers of Hindu and Sikh refugees from Pakistan arrived in their place, decisively changing the city's cultural and demographic constitution.

## 9 1984: Assassination of Indira Gandhi

The assassination of Prime Minister Indira Gandhi (1917–84) by two of her Sikh bodyguards was followed by citywide rioting. Thousands of Sikhs were killed by lynch mobs and their homes were set on fire.

## 10 2023: G20 New Delhi Summit

Delhi continues to grow economically, and recover from the crippling COVID-19 crisis. In 2023, India hosted the G20 Summit, and parts of Delhi have been refurbished to include pedestrianized streets, beautified parks and improved roads.

### TOP 10 HISTORICAL FIGURES

**1 Qutbuddin Aibak**
The Turkish slave General Qutbuddin Aibak (1150–1210) founded the Delhi Sultanate, which eventually saw 36 rulers from five separate dynasties control this region of north India.

**2 Razia Sultan**
Female sultan Razia (r 1236–40) broke every gender stereotype of her time, appearing unveiled in public and going into battle on horseback.

**3 Sher Shah Suri**
This formidable Afghan adventurer (1486–1545) wrested power from the second Mughal emperor, Humayun.

**4 Shah Jahan**
The sublime Taj Mahal was built by this Mughal emperor (1592–1666).

**5 Rani Lakshmibai of Jhansi**
The young, widowed queen of Jhansi (1828–58) who rode out to battle the British in 1857.

**6 Bahadur Shah Zafar II**
The last Mughal emperor, Bahadur Shah Zafar II (1775–1862), was the figurehead of the 1857 Uprising.

**7 Mirza Ghalib**
Ghalib (1797–1869) was the Urdu language's greatest poet, known particularly for his *ghazals (see p63)*.

**8 Edwin Lutyens**
This British architect (1869–1944) designed much of New Delhi.

**9 Sarojini Naidu**
A brilliant poet and the most well-known woman freedom fighter of India (1879–1949).

**10 Mohandas K Gandhi**
This eminent leader (1869–1948) of the Indian independence movement was assassinated in Delhi.

**Mohandas K Gandhi**

# TOP 10 Delhi Sultanate Sights

**The modest Lal Gumbad tomb**

## 1 Lal Gumbad

MAP V2 ▪ Panchsheel Park South, off Gamal Abdel Nasser Marg ▪ Hauz Khas Metro ▪ Open 24 hrs

Built for local Sufi saint Kabiruddin Aulia in 1397, the Lal Gumbad is very similar to the earlier tomb of Ghiyasuddin Tughlaq – a cube of red sandstone, almost devoid of extraneous decoration. This is Tughlaq architecture at its most austere.

## 2 Hauz Khas

Hauz Khas or Green Park Metro

The lake in Hauz Khas was built by Alauddin Khilji in 1304 to supply water to his new city at Siri. Most of the pavilions around it were added half a century later by Feroz Shah Tughlaq, who is buried here.

## 3 Begumpuri Masjid

MAP V2 ▪ Begumpur, off Guru Govind Singh Road ▪ Hauz Khas Metro

The finest of the various Sultanate-era mosques scattered about the city, the Begumpuri Masjid is a perfect example of the austere and monumental style favoured by the Tughlaq Dynasty. The simple mosque is raised, fortress-like, above the surrounding streets, centred on a huge courtyard, with a massive gateway above the central prayer hall.

## 4 Tomb of Ghiyasuddin Tughlaq

MAP X3 ▪ Tughlaqabad ▪ Tughlaqabad Metro

This simple, yet striking, red tomb is the final resting place of one of medieval India's most powerful rulers, Ghiyasuddin Tughlaq. The tomb is an almost windowless structure with sloping sides set within a small fortified compound.

## 5 Lodi Gardens

The delicately constructed octagonal tombs of Muhammad Shah, Sikander Lodi and other sultans are dotted throughout the idyllic Lodi Gardens (see pp30–31). Their relatively small scale (and light style) illustrate the declining fortunes of the Sayyid and Lodi Dynasties.

## 6 Qutb Minar

The defining image of the Delhi Sultanate, the towering Qutb Minar (see pp24–5) is a perfect example of the simple, but grandiose, Sultanate architectural style, which was intended to symbolize both the military might of the new sultans from Afghanistan and the power of the then-newly arrived Islamic faith.

**The lofty Qutb Minar**

### 7 Khirki Masjid
MAP V3 ■ Press Enclave Road ■ Malviya Nagar Metro ■ Open sunrise–sunset daily

Another superbly atmospheric Tughlaq-era mosque that was built in the 1370s, the Khirki Masjid looks more like a labrynthine fortress than a peaceful place of worship.

### 8 Quwwat-ul-Islam
The oldest mosque in India, set in the Qutb complex (see p24), this is a fascinating study in cultural contrasts. The central courtyard, fashioned out of columns from Hindu and Jain temples that previously stood on this site, has a decidedly Hindu appearance. The magnificent screen of the prayer hall, however, is a classic work of Islamic architecture covered in Koranic inscriptions.

**Ornate columns at Quwwat-ul-Islam**

### 9 Tughlaqabad
Another monumental expression of the power of the Sultanate, the city of Tughlaqabad (see p101) was built by Ghiyasuddin Tughlaq, founder of the Tughlaq Dynasty. The massive fortified cit-adel – now largely in ruins – was built, astonishingly, in just two years.

### 10 Feroz Shah Kotla
All that remains of the great city of Ferozabad (see p88) is a walled enclosure containing the fragmentary remains of a royal palace, mosque and other struc-tures. The most eye-catching feature here is the Ashokan column, which is perched atop the citadel and dates from the 3rd century BCE.

---

**TOP 10 DELHI SULTANS**

**1 Qutbuddin Aibak**
The first Delhi sultan, Qutbuddin Aibak (1150–1210) founded the Delhi Sultanate's so-called Slave Dynasty.

**2 Iltutmish**
The son-in-law of Aibak, Iltutmish (r 1211–36) extended the territory of the Sultanate from Punjab to Bengal.

**3 Razia Sultan**
Iltutmish's daughter (r 1236–40) and historically, one of the very few women to rule an Islamic state.

**4 Alauddin Khilji**
Alauddin (r 1296–1316) was the most illustrious ruler of the Khilji Dynasty.

**5 Ghiyasuddin Tughlaq**
Ghiyasuddin Tughlaq (r 1320–24) founded the Tughlaq Dynasty.

**6 Muhammad bin Tughlaq**
Eccentric ruler (r 1325–51) who tried to relocate the capital from Delhi to Daulatabad but later moved it back.

**7 Feroz Shah Tughlaq**
Feroz Shah Tughlaq (r 1351–88) tried to repair the damage inflicted on the Sultanate by his predecessor.

**8 Khizr Khan**
Khizr Khan (r 1414–21) took advantage of the power vacuum created by Timur's invasion in 1398 to establish the Sayyid Dynasty (1414–51).

**9 Buhlul Lodi**
Punjab governor (r 1451–89) who seized power from the Sayyids, establishing the last of the Sultanate's five dynasties, the Lodi Dynasty.

**10 Sikander Lodi**
Sikander Lodi (r 1489–1517) was the last Delhi sultan. His son, Ibrahim Lodi (r 1517–26), was overthrown by the great Babur, the first of the Mughals.

**A depiction of Razia Sultan**

# 🔟 Mughal Delhi Sights

**The distinctive onion domes at Nizamuddin**

### 1 Nizamuddin

The mausoleum *(see p94)* of the Sufi saint Hazrat Nizamuddin Auliya (1238–1325) was built by Muhammad bin Tughlaq in 1325. Later tombs include those of Hazrat Inayat Khan, poet Amir Khusro and Mughal princess Jehanara Begum.

### 2 Zinat ul Masjid

Dating from the reign of Aurangzeb, this neglected architectural gem is a perfect example of Mughal architecture *(see p86)* in miniature – a scaled-down version of the Jama Masjid, with a trio of marbled onion domes sitting atop the beautifully proportioned and serene prayer hall below.

### 3 Humayun's Tomb

Humayun's Tomb *(see pp18–19)* exemplifies many of the design elements that were to become standard features of the Mughal style, including the use of red sandstone with marble inlay, enormous *iwans* and the setting of the entire tomb within a very pretty Persian-style *charbagh* garden.

### 4 Purana Qila

The oldest major Mughal monument in Delhi, the walled Purana Qila *(see p93)* was begun by Humayun and completed by his Afghan successor, Sher Shah Suri *(see p43)* after he had driven his rival into exile in Persia.

### 5 Khan-i-Khanan

This is the imposing tomb *(see p92)* of Abdur Rahim, who served as prime minister to Akbar, but later fell foul of Jahangir. It is clearly modelled on the nearby Humayun's Tomb, though its rounded shape hints at the later Taj Mahal.

### 6 Jama Masjid

India's largest mosque, Shah Jahan's Jama Masjid *(see pp16–17)* is the epitome of Mughal religious architecture: a dramatically simple combination of massive arches, domes and slender minarets, towering above the streets of Old Delhi.

### 7 Zafar Mahal

Built by the Mughal emperor Akbar Shah II in the 18th century, and the last major monument of Mughal India, the Zafar Mahal *(see p27)*

**Humayun's Tomb**

summer palace is an exercise in architectural nostalgia by an increasingly powerless, and soon to be extinguished, dynasty.

**8** **Safdarjung's Tomb**
The last major Mughal mausoleum in Delhi, Safdarjung's Tomb *(see p94)* is generally thought to exemplify the creative decline that set in following the demise of Shah Jahan, though its fanciful façades and interior lend it a certain kitsch charm entirely its own.

**9** **Red Fort**
Despite suffering considerable damage during the 1857 Uprising and afterwards, the Red Fort *(see pp12–13)* remains a treasure trove of Mughal architectural styles, with grand gateways, formal gardens and a sequence of royal pavilions strung out along the ramparts.

**Interior of Jamali-Kamali Masjid**

**10** **Jamali-Kamali Masjid**
Completed in 1536 during Humayun's first reign *(see p19)*, the simple but elegant Jamali-Kamali Masjid *(see p26)* is Delhi's finest example of early-Mughal architecture.

**TOP 10 MUGHAL DESIGN FEATURES**

**Floral *pietra dura* tilework**

**1 *Pietra Dura***
A hallmark of the Shah Jahan-era style, where colourful gemstones are embedded in white marble to create elaborate floral or abstract designs.

**2 *Iwans***
Huge central arches providing a focus on the façades of tombs and mosques.

**3 Cusped Arches**
Staple of Mughal architecture, derived from Rajasthani and Bengali styles.

**4 Red Sandstone and White Marble**
A classic Mughal combination: façades of red sandstone that are decorated with bands of white marble inlay.

**5 *Jalis***
Delicately carved marble or sandstone screens, often used to enclose tombs.

**6 Tilework**
A technique derived from Persia, using coloured tiles (usually, but not exclusively, blue) to decorate domes, window frames and façades.

**7 *Charbagh* Gardens**
Persian-style gardens, divided by water channels into four equal quadrants.

**8 Domes**
Distinctive Persian-style onion domes, often crowned with dramatic finials.

**9 *Chhatris***
Small, domed pavilions supported on four pillars, common in Hindu architecture and used on the eaves and minarets of Mughal buildings.

**10 *Jharokas***
Distinctive balconied windows, often richly carved – another classic Hindu feature adopted by the Mughals.

# TOP 10 Monuments of the 1857 Uprising

**Daily prayers at Fatehpuri Masjid**

### 1 Fatehpuri Masjid

This Chandni Chowk mosque (see p15) was a hotbed of religious fervour and nationalist sentiment during the 1857 Uprising. The British responded by sacking the mosque and selling it to a local businessman, although two decades later they bought it back and returned it to Delhi's Muslim community. A number of Indian soldiers killed in the uprising lie buried in the courtyard.

### 2 Flagstaff Tower

**MAP B4** ■ Magazine Road, Northern Ridge ■ Vidhan Sabha Metro

Built in 1828 as a British signalling post, the tower served as a shelter for dozens of civilians fleeing the city after the outbreak of hostilities during the 1857 Uprising.

**The exterior of Flagstaff Tower**

### 3 Mutiny Monument

**MAP E1** ■ Rani Jhansi Road ■ Pul Bangash Metro

This grandiose Gothic-style Victorian monument, built in 1863, commemorates the British soldiers (and "native" troops in British employ) killed during the uprising, with panels listing the names, ranks and numbers of military fatalities. An additional panel, added in 1972, offers an Indian perspective on the events described and is worth a look.

### 4 British Residency

**MAP H2** ■ Sham Nath Marg ■ Kashmiri Gate Metro

The old Neo-Classical British Residency was built around the ruins of a Mughal library erected by Dara Shikoh (1615–59), son of Shah Jahan. It is now home to the Archaeology Department of the Guru Gobind Singh Indraprastha University.

### 5 Northern Ridge

**MAP E1** ■ Rani Jhansi Road ■ Pul Bangash, Vidhan Sabha Metro

North of Old Delhi, the Aravalli Range forms a long, low ridge. This is where the refugees from Delhi converged during the 1857 Uprising, and where British forces gathered before launching an assault to recapture the city.

### **6** St James' Church

This beautiful colonial-era church *(see p85)* holds a number of memorials to British civilians killed in Delhi during the 1857 Uprising. It also contains a memorial to the Reverend Midgeley John Jennings, then chaplain of Delhi, whose rather high-handed Christian evangelizing did much to enflame local religious sensibilities, and who was killed in the Red Fort during the first few hours of the revolt.

### **7** Magazine
**MAP H2 ▪ Sham Nath Marg ▪ Kashmiri Gate Metro**

Now marooned on a traffic island, this small British magazine was at the heart of the first day of fighting in Delhi. Surrounded by enemy Indian sepoys, the British troops stationed inside the magazine decided to blow it up rather than allow its stock of arms and ammunition to fall into Indian hands. The explosion killed around 400 sepoys and onlookers.

### **8** Kashmiri Gate
**MAP G2 ▪ Sham Nath Marg ▪ Kashmiri Gate Metro**

Now dwarfed by the vast new Kashmiri Gate Metro, this modest little Mughal-era gateway witnessed the most bitter fighting of the entire uprising, when British troops stormed the gate in order to force a route into the rebel-held city. A plaque at the rear commemorates those who were killed in the assault.

The Lal Darwaza or Bloody Gate

### **9** Lal Darwaza
**MAP H6 ▪ Mathura Road ▪ Pragati Maidan Metro**

The red sandstone Lal Darwaza (also known as the Khooni Darwaza, or Bloody Gate) marks the site of one of the most notorious episodes of the uprising *(see p43)*, when British officer William Hodson summarily executed Mirza Mughal, Kizr Sultan and Abu Bakr, sons and grandson, respectively, of the last Mughal emperor.

### **10** Nicholson's Cemetery

Tucked away in Old Delhi, this atmospheric and rambling colonial-era cemetery *(see p88)* is a haven from the chaotic hustle and bustle of the old city. Beautifully restored in 2006, it is the final resting place of hundreds of India's early European inhabitants. Of its many graves, monuments and tombs, the most famous is that of Brigadier-General John Nicholson (1822–57), a prominent British army commander and one of the key figures in the history of the 1857 Uprising – he is best known for planning and leading the final British assault on Delhi. Nicholson was killed in September 1857 during the bitter fighting that took place for the recapture of the city.

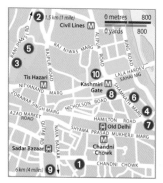

# 🔟 Cities of Delhi, Old and New

### 2 Lal Kot and Qila Rai Pithora

The first of Delhi's traditional seven cities, Lal Kot was established by a Rajput clan, the Tomars, in 1060. A century later, they became vassals of the Chauhans, who extended Lal Kot and renamed it Qila Rai Pithora. Both settlements were largely buried under the Qutb Minar (see pp24–5) complex.

### 3 Siri
**MAP V2**

The second city of Delhi, Siri was built during the reign of Alauddin Khilji (see p43). These days little remains of it, barring a few sections of the walls. More impressive is the water tank Alauddin built nearby at Hauz Khas (see p100) to supply water to Siri. It was later expanded by Feroz Shah Tughlaq (r 1351–88).

### 1 Indraprastha

The legendary city of Indraprastha, home of the Pandava brothers of the epic *Mahabharata*, is said to have stood on the site that is now occupied by the Purana Qila. Conclusive evidence is sadly lacking, although finds have been unearthed here dating to the 3rd century BCE, and an ancient village stood here until the early 20th century. Today this is home to one of the oldest forts in Delhi and is a great place to visit.

### 4 Tuqhlaqabad

Built during the reign of Ghiyasuddin Tughlaq (r 1320–24), Tughlaqabad (see p101), the third city of Delhi, was quickly abandoned. The city's most impressive features are the massive fortified citadel and ramparts, stretching for over 6 km (4 miles), and the distinctive tomb of Ghiyasuddin himself. A smaller subsidiary fortress, known as Adilabad, stands nearby.

**The ancient ruined citadel and ramparts of Tuqhlaqabad**

The buildings of the Central Secretariat in New Delhi

 **5 Jahanpanah**

Delhi's fourth city, Jahanpanah, was built by Muhammad bin Tughlaq *(see p43)* shortly before the eccentric ruler briefly abandoned Delhi for the city of Daulatabad. Two important monuments survive here: the Bijay Mandal, which is thought to be Tughlaq's palace, as well as the Begumpuri Mosque *(see p100)*.

**6 Ferozabad**

Constructed by Feroz Shah Tughlaq, Ferozabad was the fifth city of Delhi. Today, the principal surviving structure is the walled palace known as Feroz Shah Kotla *(see p88)*, its crumbling remains topped by one of the city's two Ashokan pillars *(see p88)*.

**7 Purana Qila**

Built on the fabled site of Indraprastha, Purana Qila – the sixth city of Delhi – was begun by the second Mughal emperor Humayun *(see p19)* and completed by his great rival Sher Shah Suri *(see p43)*. Following Suri's death, Humayun reclaimed the Purana Qila *(see p93)*, but died within a year after falling down a steep flight of steps.

**8 Shahjahanabad**

Begun by Shah Jahan in 1638, Shahjahanabad (Old Delhi) was the last of Delhi's so-called seven cities. It was intended to provide North India with a capital to replace Agra.

**9 New Delhi**

Built in 1911–1931, the city of New Delhi was an attempt by the British to assert their Imperial credentials, featuring showpiece architectural landmarks including the Secretariat Buildings and the Rashtrapati Bhavan *(see p21)*. Edwin Lutyens was asked to create a city that would rival the great cities of the Mughals and the Delhi sultans and legitimize Britain's increasingly shaky hold on the country.

**10 Satellite Cities**

Thanks to the metro, Delhi's satellite towns have become more accessible and are attracting corporations and wealthy residents. To the south, Gurugram (formerly Gurgaon) is a city of gleaming high-rises, many the headquarters of IT companies. Noida in the east, is another shiny steel-and-glass IT hub.

The town of Gurugram at night

# 🔟 Places of Worship

**The Baha'i Temple, popularly known as the Lotus Temple**

## 1 Baha'i Temple
This remarkable building *(see p99)* – an abstract composition inspired by the shape of an unfurling lotus flower – was built in 1986 by the Baha'is and is open to everyone. Founded by 19th-century Persian visionary Baha'u'llah, this is the main temple of the Baha'i faith in India and is one of the most visited monuments in the world. The religion believes in the unity of all religions and people.

**The colonial-style St James' Church**

## 2 St James' Church
One of the city's oldest churches *(see p85)*, this architectural gem was built by the legendary Anglo-Indian soldier James Skinner (1778–1841). Barred from serving in the British army owing to his mixed race, Skinner established his own irregular cavalry regiment, Skinner's Horse, which forms a part of the Indian army to this day.

## 3 Gurudwara Bangla Sahib
Built in 1783 in honour of the eighth Sikh Guru Har Krishan, this *(see p80)* is the city's largest Sikh temple. The guru visited Delhi in 1664 during a cholera and smallpox epidemic, tending to the sick and offering them fresh water from the *sarovar* (lake) on the site, which is still believed to possess medicinal properties.

## 4 Zinat ul Masjid
Popularly known as the Ghata (Cloud) Masjid *(see p86)*, this beautiful building was commissioned by Aurangzeb's daughter Zinat ul Nisa and was completed in 1707. It is one of the city's only Mughal monuments grand enough to rival Shah Jahan's earlier creations.

## 5 Lakshmi Narayan Mandir
This eye-catching Hindu temple *(see p79)*, popularly known as Birla Mandir, was commissioned by industrialist B D Birla and consecrated in 1939 by Gandhi – one of the first temples in India open to everyone, irrespective of caste. The spacious interior is centred on a shrine to Lakshmi and her consort Narayan (Vishnu), flanked by images of Durga and Shiva.

## 6 Nizamuddin
One of the most magical places in Delhi, the wonderfully atmospheric religious complex

of Nizamuddin *(see p94)* grew up around the revered *dargah* (Muslim shrine) of the Chishti Sufi saint Nizamuddin Auliya. Among the cluster of structures now surrounding the saint's tomb are the Jamat Khana Masjid (1325) and the graves of the famous poet Amir Khusrau (1253–1325) and Princess Jahanara, Shah Jahan's daughter.

### 7 Lal Mandir

This Jain temple *(see p14)* is one of the city's most important. Topped by a cluster of towers, made of red Kota stone, it has a richly painted interior, full of diminutive marble images of various Jain gurus in glass cases. Next to the temple is a small "bird hospital", where birds are fed and cared for – evidence of the profound respect that the Jain religion has for all forms of life.

**Akshardham Temple**

### 8 Akshardham Temple

This gargantuan modern Hindu temple *(see p94)*, inaugurated in 2005, was built in honour of the sage Bhagwan Shri Swaminarayan (1781–1830), who left his birthplace in Uttar Pradesh at the age of 11 and walked for seven years and 12,000 km (7,456 miles) before establishing an *ashram* (hermitage) in Gujarat. From here, he preached a message of nonviolence and spiritual unity, attracting many Hindu followers as well as Muslim and Zoroastrian devotees.

**Jama Masjid, India's largest mosque**

### 9 Begumpuri Masjid

Built in the 1340s by Muhammad bin Tughlaq as part of his city of Jahanpanah, this little-visited mosque *(see p100)* is one of the finest in Delhi. The mosque is centred on a huge courtyard surrounded by domed arcades, with a fortress-like gateway leading into the prayer hall – a perfect example of Tughlaq architecture at its rugged and imposing best.

### 10 Jama Masjid

Delhi's spectacular Jama Masjid *(see pp16–17)*, the second largest in the subcontinent, is a key centre for Islamic worship. Shah Jahan's final architectural triumph, it can hold a staggering 25,000 people.

# 🔟 Museums and Galleries

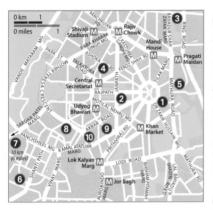

### 4 National Philatelic Museum

Heaven for stamp enthusiasts, the National Philatelic Museum (see p80) holds a copy of every Indian stamp produced since independence (around 1,700 issues), an interesting selection of international stamps and the personal belongings of a mid-19th-century postman.

### 5 National Crafts Museum

This museum (see pp28–9) is another of Delhi's must-see cultural attractions, showcasing a variety of artifacts inspired by the country's Indigenous folk-art traditions. Exhibits include detailed ivory carvings, as well as a vast collection of textiles and fabrics and Hindu bronzes, while outside in the grounds you can see a set of traditional buildings from all around India.

### 1 National Gallery of Modern Art (NGMA)

Set in Jaipur House, the former residence of the Jaipur royals, the NGMA displays works from 1857, including those by the founders of modern art in India such as Rabindranath Tagore, Raja Ravi Verma and Amrita Sher-Gil. There's a separate wing dedicated to special exhibitions and a conservatory laboratory.

### 2 National Museum

The National Museum (see pp32–5) is an obligatory stop on any tour of Delhi's museums. It has a superb array of exhibits covering every epoch in the country's history, ranging from priceless Indus Valley artifacts to Chola bronzes and Mughal miniatures.

### 6 National Rail Museum

India's love affair with the railway is celebrated in this fine museum (see p95) containing assorted antique steam engines and opulent carriages, including those once belonging to the maharajas of Mysore and Baroda, and the Prince of Wales.

### 3 National Gandhi Museum

The city's second Gandhi museum (see p88) is close to Raj Ghat where the Father of the Nation was cremated. Exhibits on display include Gandhi's memorabilia and that of his wife, plus six telephones on which visitors can listen to his famous speeches in Hindi and English.

**Antique train at National Rail Museum**

**Gandhi Smriti, where Gandhi spent the last days of his life**

### 7 Sulabh International Museum of Toilets

MAP A5 ■ Mahavir Enclave, Palam Dabri Marg ■ 2503 1518 ■ Uttam Nagar East Metro ■ Open 10am–5pm Mon–Sat ■ www.sulabh toiletmuseum.org

Although this museum may sound like a joke, it has quite a serious purpose, being part of the neo-Gandhian Sulabh International Movement, which aims to promote public hygiene, with many displays on lavatorial habits.

### 8 Pradhanmantri Sangrahalaya

Teen Murti House, formerly called Flagstaff House, was built in 1930 as the residence of the British military commander-in-chief and later became home to India's first Prime Minister Jawaharlal Nehru (1889–1964). This renovated and refurbished classic Lutyens-style building has now been seamlessly incorporated into the Pradhanmantri Sangrahalaya, a museum dedicated to every prime minister of India since independence.

### 9 Gandhi Smriti

Formerly known as Birla House, this Neo-Classical mansion (see p79) is where Gandhi (1869–1948) spent the last 144 days of his life. Displays include a touching

**Sulabh International Museum of Toilets**

collection of the Mahatma's personal belongings, such as the watch he was wearing when he was assasinated, which stopped at the moment of his death.

### 10 Indira Gandhi Memorial Museum

This museum (see p78) is the former home of Prime Minister Indira Gandhi (1917–84), who was assassinated in the garden here by two of her Sikh bodyguards. The absorbing exhibits include personal belongings and photos, plus a section devoted to her son Rajiv (1944–91), including the shoes he was wearing when he was killed by Tamil separatists in 1991.

**Exhibits at Indira Gandhi Memorial**

# ᴛᴏᴘ10 Delhi-Inspired Books

**Indian author Anita Desai**

malls and tranquil gardens while trying to fathom some logic in the chaos that abounds.

### ④ Trees of Delhi: A Field Guide (Pradip Krishen)

With a total ban on high-rise constructions still effective across large parts of the capital, Delhi's skyline is dominated not just by buildings but by trees. Ecologist and tree-lover Pradip Krishen's field guide provides an excellent introduction to some of the common varieties of trees that dot the city which, by many accounts, has become greener over recent years.

### ⑤ The Delhi Omnibus (introduction by Narayani Gupta)

This omnibus captures not just the physical history of the city, but the manner in which the people have invented and reinvented themselves over time. It contains writings by Percival Spear, Narayani Gupta, R E Frykenberg and Christopher Bayly.

### ⑥ Delhi: Adventures in a Megacity (Sam Miller)

A very entertaining eye-witness account of contemporary Delhi, this book follows a spiralling perambulation through the city, from the centre of Connaught Place out into the suburbs, with wonderfully evocative descriptions of the many people and places encountered on the journey.

*Delhi: Adventures in a Megacity*

### ① Clear Light of Day (Anita Desai)

This is Anita Desai's most obviously autobiographical work, centred on the contrasting stories of two sisters from Old Delhi – one of whom leaves the city and the other of whom remains – and their subsequent reunion.

### ② The White Tiger (Aravind Adiga)

A Booker Prize-winning debut novel by Chennai-born Aravind Adiga, this is partly set in Delhi, and relates the murderous career of anti-hero Balram Halwai, with insights into contemporary Indian society en route.

### ③ Delirious Delhi (Dave Prager)

Two New Yorkers dive deep into the capital's frantic energy, volume and humour, visiting ancient monuments, modern

### ⑦ Delhi: A Novel (Khushwant Singh)

This is an engaging novel by one of India's foremost modern writers.

Historical snapshots of the city through the ages – culminating in the anti-Sikh riots of 1984 – are interspersed with a secondary narrative about a journalist and the passionate relationship he develops with a *hijra* (eunuch).

### ⑧ City of Djinns (William Dalrymple)

A beautifully written portrait of Delhi's multilayered personality, this book is particularly strong on the city's history, interspersed with richly comic snapshots of the modern city.

### ⑨ Twilight in Delhi (Ahmed Ali)

A novel by Delhi-born Ahmed Ali, this paints a beautiful portrait of the city at the beginning of the 20th century – an elegiac lament for the city's rapidly disappearing Mughal traditions in the face of the Colonial and European cultural onslaught.

### ⑩ Corridor (Sarnath Banerjee)

This graphic novel showcases Delhi through the eyes of a second-hand bookseller in Connaught Place and avoids the usual clichés associated with the city.

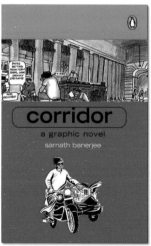

*Corridor* **by Sarnath Banerjee**

## TOP 10 FILMS BASED IN DELHI

**Poster art for *Monsoon Wedding***

**1 Fire (1996)**
A controversial tale of a lesbian affair between two Delhi housewives.

**2 Monsoon Wedding (2001)**
Mira Nair's marvellously evocative portrait of the people and places of contemporary Delhi, combining social comedy with stunning cinematography.

**3 Rang De Basanti (2006)**
An influential film by director Rakeysh Omprakash Mehra about five young men who are trying to expose India's widespread political corruption.

**4 Delhi-6 (2009)**
A Rakeysh Omprakash Mehra film depicting the lives and loves of an eclectic array of Old Delhi characters.

**5 Dev.D (2009)**
Clever, contemporary reworking of the classic Bengali movie *Devdas*.

**6 Delhi Belly (2011)**
A black comedy, starring Imran Khan, about three friends who share a room in Delhi and somehow get involved in an underworld crime plot.

**7 No One Killed Jessica (2011)**
Based on the real-life shooting of a bartender by a politician's son and her sister's struggle for justice.

**8 Pink (2016)**
A gripping legal thriller that reflects the status of women in society, with a message on the importance of consent.

**9 Hindi Medium (2017)**
A comedy drama that centres on the challenges of obtaining a good "English medium" education.

**10 Batla House (2019)**
This action-packed movie is inspired by true events that involved an encounter with terrorists at Delhi's Batla House.

# 🔟 Parks and Gardens

**Statue at Buddha Jayanti Park**

## 1 Buddha Jayanti Park
**MAP K2 ■ Vandemataram Marg ■ Jhandewalan Metro ■ Open 5am–7pm daily**
Hemmed in amidst the woodland of the Ridge west of New Delhi, this beautiful park was created in 1993 to mark the 2,500th anniversary of the Buddha's enlightenment. A Buddha statue sits within the park.

## 2 Lodi Gardens
This is one of the most picturesque gardens (see pp30–31) in Delhi, with idyllic lawns and shady patches of woodland dotted with the imposing tombs of assorted Lodi and Sayyid rulers and nobles.

## 3 Amrit Udyan
Amrit Udyan (see p21), previously known as the Mughal Gardens, is open to the public only for a month in spring. Designed by Edwin Lutyens in a blend of Mughal and English styles, it has many rare species of flora, including 250 types of roses and 60 types of bougainvilleas.

## 4 Sunder Nursery
**MAP R5 ■ Off Mathura Road ■ JLN, Khan Market Metro ■ Open 7am–10pm daily**
This heritage park complex, known as Azim Bagh in Mughal times, lies adjacent to Humayun's Tomb (see p18). It includes many 16th-century monuments and a biodiversity park with flora specific to Delhi.

## 5 Qudsia Bagh
North of Old Delhi lies Qudsia Bagh (see p88), created in 1748 as a royal pleasure park by Qudsia Begum (1801–81), wife of Mughal emperor Muhammad Shah. Little survives of the park's original buildings apart from a gateway and a mosque at the garden's southeastern end.

## 6 Talkatora Gardens
**MAP L2 ■ Mother Teresa Crescent ■ Open sunrise–sunset daily**
Behind Rashtrapati Bhavan, these 18th-century gardens are among central Delhi's most popular parks. They are prettiest in spring when the colourful shrubs burst into life.

## 7 Garden of Five Senses
**MAP V3 ■ Said-ul-Ajaib village, near Mahavirsthal on the Mehrauli–Badarpur Road ■ Saket Metro ■ Open Apr–Sep: 9am–7pm daily (Oct–Mar: until 6pm) ■ Adm**
Dotted with sculptures, the Garden of Five Senses is divided into various landscaped areas, with sensory themes and names such as the "Trail of Fragrance" and "Colour Gardens".

### 8 Nehru Park
MAP L6 ■ Panchsheel Road, Chanyakapuri ■ Open 5am–8pm daily

Nehru Park is one of the most popular retreats in South Delhi, with spacious lawns, a pool and an open-air gym with fitness equipment.

### 9 Raj Ghat
These gardens *(see p85)* are best known as the place where the funeral rites of modern India's most important leaders took place, including Mahatma Gandhi, Indira Gandhi, Rajiv Gandhi and Jawaharlal Nehru, each of whom is commemorated with a monument.

**Mahatma Gandhi memorial, Raj Ghat**

### 10 Coronation Park
MAP B4 ■ Shanti Swaroop Tyagi Marg, near Nirankari Sarovar ■ Open sunrise–sunset daily

North of Connaught Place, this was the site of the three British Durbars of 1887, 1903 and 1911. The statue of King George V was moved here from the canopy in India Gate in the 1960s. The park has since been redeveloped with a focus on the towering Coronation Memorial.

**Amrit Udyan**

**TOP 10 INDIAN TREES**

**The flowers of the gulmohar tree**

**1 Gulmohar (*Delonix regia*)**
The Indian flame tree has distinctive fern-like leaves and bright red flowers.

**2 Neeli Gulmohar (*Jacaranda mimosifolia*)**
The jacaranda is a flowering tree, which explodes in spring into a very distinctive purple-blue blossom.

**3 Peepul (*Ficus religiosa*)**
A species of banyan fig, this is also Buddhism's sacred tree (commonly known as the bodhi tree).

**4 Amaltas (*Cassia fistula*)**
A shrub (Indian laburnum in English) with Ayurvedic properties, this bursts into cascading yellow flowers in spring.

**5 Champa (*Plumeria rubra*)**
A species of frangipani, this is one of the most common Indian flowering shrubs, producing huge white blooms.

**6 Semal (*Bombax ceiba*)**
The red silk cotton tree is an attractive ornamental tree and especially pretty in spring, when it is covered in vibrant red flowers, with no leaves.

**7 Jamun (*Syzygium cumini*)**
The evergreen black plum is known for its large purple berries. It also features in the epic, the *Ramayana*.

**8 Kachnar (*Bauhinia variegata*)**
The popular ornamental orchid tree has scented pink or white flowers.

**9 Dhak (*Butea monosperma*)**
This pretty flowering species, known as the flame of the forest in English, has curved, bright orange flowers.

**10 Neem (*Azadirachta indica*)**
A common South Asian tree (Indian lilac), the neem is renowned for its medicinal properties, hence its popular description as the "village pharmacy".

# **TOP 10** Off the Beaten Track

### 1 Shankar's International Dolls Museum

MAP H6 ■ 4 Bahadur Shah Zafar Marg ■ 2331 6970 ■ Open 10am–5:30pm Tue–Sun ■ Adm ■ www.childrensbooktrust.com/dolls museum.html

Doll enthusiasts will love this prodigious collection of over 6,000 dolls from around the world, many dressed in regional and national costumes, and including amusing mannequins of John Wayne, Louis Armstrong and Henry VIII.

### 2 Majnu ka Tila

MAP B4 ■ Aruna Nagar, Outer Ring Road ■ 15 min walk or short auto-rickshaw ride from Vidhan Sabha Metro

Here in Delhi's little Tibet the Dalai Lama's image beams down from the wall of almost every establishment. Visitors can buy prayer wheels, *thangkas* (traditional Buddhist religious paintings) and books about Tibet, and enjoy Tibetan food.

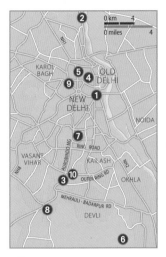

**Prayer wheels, Majnu ka Tila**

### 3 Adhchini

MAP V2 ■ Qutab Enclave, Aurobindo Marg ■ Hauz Khas Metro

An urban village, with residents, who mainly belong to a community called the Jats, Adhchini contains a 16th-century Lodi mosque and an impressive shrine to the mother of Nizamuddin Auliya *(see p94).*

### 4 Kalan Masjid

MAP G5 ■ In an alley opposite 2063 Mohammed Deen Haichi Marg ■ Tikri Kalan Metro

Built in 1387, this blue-and-green mosque, located near Turkman Gate, was – along with Khirki Masjid *(see p45)* – one of seven mosques commissioned by Feroz Shah's chief minister Khan-i-Jahan Junan Shah. It is the only one still in use today.

### 5 Masjid Mubarak Begum

MAP G4 ■ 4959 Hauz Razi, Lalkuan Bazaar Road ■ Chawri Bazaar Metro

This private mosque was built in 1823 for the Indian wife of Sir David Ochterlony, British Resident at the Mughal Court. Hidden away above a busy bazaar, and accessed by a narrow stairway between two shops (guests must take their shoes off at the top), it has a tiny prayer hall with enough room for ten worshippers.

### 6 Surajkund Dam
Anangpur, 20 km (12 miles)
S of central Delhi, 4 km (2 miles)
W of NHPC Chowk metro station
■ Surajkund Tank: open sunrise–
sunset daily ■ Adm

Way off the beaten track, but still
within easy reach of the metro, this
is Delhi's oldest construction, built
under the Tomar king Anangpal in
the 8th century to store rainwater
for irrigation. Surajkund Tank, 2 km
(1 mile) to its north, is an ancient
10th-century reservoir, which was
also built under the Tomars.

### 7 Aliganj
MAP N7 ■ Between Aliganj
Road and Karbala Road, Jor Bagh
■ Jor Bagh Metro ■ www.shahe
mardan.org

Once the estate of the Shiite rulers
of Awadh, the family of the Nawab of
Safdarjung, this area has interesting
18th-century buildings. Most notable
among these is the Shah-e-Mardan
Dargah, a Shia shrine where Sunnis
and some Hindus go to pray.

### 8 Chhattarpur Mandir
MAP B7 ■ Main Chhattarpur
Road ■ 2680 2925 ■ Chhattarpur
Metro ■ Open 6am–10pm daily

This was the biggest temple in India
when it was built in 1974, but it is
really a park-like compound with
several temples inside it, presided
over by a 30-m (98-ft) high statue
of the monkey god, Hanuman. The
complex was financed by followers
of a guru known as Babaji, whose
ashes rest in one of the temples.

**Paharganj Christian Cemetery**

### 9 Paharganj Christian Cemetery
MAP E5 ■ Ramdwara Road, Nehru
Bazaar ■ 2358 5710 ■ Open daily

It is easy to forget that Christianity
is an important religion in India,
where three states still have Christian
majorities. This cemetery has
faithfully served Delhi's Christian
community since the 19th century,
but really comes to life on Halloween,
when it sparkles with candles left
by relatives visiting the deceased.

### 10 Bijay Mandal
MAP V2 ■ Kalu Sarai, near
Hauz Khas Metro

Around 100 m (330 ft) north of
Begumpuri Masjid (see p100), this
atmospheric ruin is all that remains
of Sultan Muhammad bin Tughlaq's
palace. Visitors can climb to the
octagonal pavilion on its roof for
great views over the city.

**The Chhattarpur Mandir complex**

# 🔟 Performing Arts Venues

**Classical dance performance during a show at Kamani Auditorium**

### ① Kamani Auditorium

MAP Q1 ■ Mandi House, 1 Copernicus Marg ■ 4350 3351 ■ Mandi House Metro ■ www. kamaniauditorium.org

The Kamani Auditorium is one of the city's leading venues for classical music and dance, attracting leading performers from across the country.

### ② Triveni Kala Sangam

MAP G7 ■ 205 Tansen Marg ■ 2371 8833 ■ Mandi House Metro ■ www. trivenikalasangam.org

This cultural centre houses a range of venues, including galleries, an auditorium and an open-air theatre.

### ③ Shri Ram Centre for Performing Arts

MAP Q1 ■ 4 Safdar Hashmi Marg ■ 2371 4307 ■ Mandi House Metro ■ www.shriram centre.org

Established in 1975, this is an important theatrical venue, staging a wide range of interesting productions that include musical, traditional and experimental theatre.

**Theatre artist at NSD**

### ④ Sangeet Natak Akademi

MAP P1 ■ Rabindra Bhavan, 35 Feroz Shah Road ■ 2338 7246 ■ Mandi House Metro ■ www. sangeetnatak.gov.in

This is one of the country's foremost performing arts venues, and home to Delhi's finest open-air theatre. It also has a library and a gallery featuring a range of traditional musical instruments, masks and puppets.

### ⑤ National School of Drama (NSD)

MAP Q1 ■ Bahawalpur House, 1 Bhagwan Das Road ■ 2338 9402 ■ Mandi House Metro ■ www. nsd.gov.in

The National School of Drama (NSD) is the country's leading academy for aspiring actors. The productions are staged by current students and the school's professional repertory company.

### ⑥ Akshara Theatre

MAP M1 ■ Baba Kharak Singh Marg ■ RK Ashram, Patel Chowk and Rajiv Chowk metros ■ www. aksharatheatre.com

This lovely arts complex in the heart of New Delhi has regular shows of classic and contemporary theatre.

## 7 India International Centre

MAP P6 ▪ 40 Max Mueller Marg ▪ 2461 9431 ▪ www.iicdelhi.nic.in

Besides regular music, dance and theatrical performances, the India International Centre (IIC) hosts exhibitions and talks attracting leading cultural personalities, both national and international. It also hosts a popular cinema club with art-house film screenings.

## 8 Nizamuddin

The fascinating religious enclave of Nizamuddin *(see p94)* is Delhi's most atmospheric venue for impromptu music, with nightly performances of ecstatic qawwali singing around the shrine of Nizamuddin Auliya, the famous Sufi saint.

## 9 Siri Fort

MAP V2 ▪ Khel Gaon Marg ▪ 2649 3370 ▪ Green Park Metro

The extensive Siri Fort Cultural Complex features three auditoriums (the largest seating almost 2,000 people), staging a range of big-name events, particularly Indian classical music concerts, dance and film.

## 10 India Habitat Centre (IHC)

MAP P6 ▪ Lodi Road ▪ 2468 2001/2009 ▪ www.indiahabitat.org

This is one of Delhi's state-of-the-art performing-arts venues, and hosts regular music, dance and cultural events such as art-house film screenings and talks.

**A literary festival at the IHC**

---

**TOP 10 FORMS OF INDIAN CLASSICAL MUSIC**

**A party of qawwali singers**

**1 Qawwali**
Sufi devotional music, with ecstatic, rhythmic singing used by devotees to achieve the trance-like state that Sufis believe brings them closer to God.

**2 Dhrupad**
One of the oldest and most austere forms of Hindustani classical vocal music, said to have developed from the chanting of Vedic hymns.

**3 Thumri**
A type of love song, usually performed in Braj Bhasha, a dialect of Hindi.

**4 Dadra**
A light form of Hindustani classical vocal music popular in north India.

**5 Tarana**
North Indian vocal genre involving the rapid singing of musical syllables based on Persian/Arabic phonemes.

**6 Kriti**
The major vocal genre of Carnatic music, divided into three parts, and with a religious theme.

**7 Varnam**
Form of Carnatic vocal music designed to bring out the qualities of the underlying raga.

**8 Padam**
Light classical love songs in the Carnatic tradition, often sung during Bharatanatyam dance performances.

**9 Ghazal**
Persian-derived light classical song form, often using lyrics by Urdu poets.

**10 Raga and Khayal**
The system of modes underlying all Indian classical music, a framework for composition and improvisation. A *khayal* is the extended, improvised elaboration of a raga using a lyrical composition called a *bandish*.

# TOP 10 Places to Eat

### 1 Olive Bar & Kitchen

Located in the rustic yet swanky One Style Mile, Olive Bar & Kitchen *(see p105)* is one of the prettiest restaurants in town, with a lovely, airy courtyard and the Qutb Minar providing a stunning back-drop. The food here, mainly Mediterranean, Indian and Italian, is delicious too.

**Indian Accent fusion cuisine**

### 2 SodaBottleOpenerWala

Straight out of Bombay but with a strong Iranian influence, this restaurant *(see p97)* specializes in the food of the Parsi community. As well as *dhansak*, there are more adventurous dishes such as sweet-and-sour brinjal *patio* or the berry *pulao*, made famous by Bombay's Britannia restaurant. Baked goodies include ginger biscuit and *mawa* cake.

### 3 Chor Bizarre

This place *(see p89)* specializes in excellent Kashmiri dishes rarely found elsewhere, such as *goshtaba* (slow-cooked mutton in yoghurt and cardamon) and a wonderful Kashmiri version of *dum aloo*. The decor is delightfully eccentric.

### 4 Indian Accent

A superb modern Indian fusion restaurant *(see p97)*, where the dishes run from paneer tikka quesadillas and tofu coriander *vadas* to tandoori bacon prawns. It can be difficult to make a decision with the range of innovative local dishes on offer so it's worth checking out the excellent vegetarian and non-vegetarian tasting menus on offer.

### 5 Saravana Bhavan

An excellent and inexpensive south Indian vegetarian restaurant *(see p83)*, where diners can feast on *idli sambar*, *masala dosa* and many other regional specialities, or tuck into a tasty vegetarian *thali*. If that is too filling, visitors can go for the mini tiffin, which offers a small taste of everything on the menu.

### 6 Spice Route

Housed in The Imperial, Spice Route *(see p83)* offers guests a special dining experience. The cuisine is from southeast Asia and the Indian state of Kerala – it is fiery, and the emphasis is on fish and seafood. A tasting menu is available in the evenings.

**Diners at the whimsically decorated Chor Bizarre**

###  House of Ming

This is a stylish restaurant *(see p83)* that recreates an ambience reminiscent of the Ming dynasty. The menu celebrates Szechuan, Cantonese and Hunan cuisine with an array of innovative dishes that make for an exceptional fine dining experience.

**Table setting at Bukhara**

###  Bukhara

With a guest list that includes former US President Bill Clinton, Bukhara *(see p97)* offers a rich menu that includes the city's best-loved dishes. The buttery *dal bukhara* (lentils) is legendary, as is the melt-in-the-mouth lamb dish and the *Sikandari raan* (mutton leg roast).

### The China Kitchen

A far cry from the usual Indian-influenced Chinese fare served up in the city, the food in The China Kitchen *(see p105)* is modern and experimental yet deeply rooted in traditional, primarily Szechuan, flavours. Diners swear the Peking Duck is the best in Delhi.

### Karim's

Headed by a line of chefs that, apparently, used to prepare meals for Mughal emperors, Karim's *(see p89)* is arguably the city's most famous restaurant. Try the excellent mutton *korma* and *seekh kebabs*.

---

### TOP 10 BARS AND NIGHTCLUBS

**1 PCO**
A "speakeasy" *(see p103)* featuring retro decor and a well-stocked bar serving cocktails. Requires a secret code – periodically changed – for entry.

**2 Kitty Su**
This colourful nightclub *(see p82)* off Connaught Place has a vibrant atmosphere and hosts concerts and events.

**3 1911**
A quiet, elegant Art Deco place, 1911 *(see p82)* is steeped in old-world charm.

**4 Rick's**
Sample the many wines and cocktails at this urban lounge bar *(see p82)*.

**5 Social**
Offering all-day breakfast and signature drinks such as the Aacharoska (caipiroska with Indian lime pickle), this café-bar *(see p103)* is a must visit.

**6 Monkey Bar**
Fun and quirky, this Indian-inspired gastropub *(see p103)* serves innovative dishes and cocktails.

**7 Fio Cookhouse & Bar**
Great thin-crust pizzas and potent cocktails with a twist are available here *(see p105)*.

**8 G-Bar**
MAP T2 ▪ The Grand, Nelson Mandela Marg ▪ 2677 1234 ▪ Open 6pm–3am daily
This bar attracts a young crowd with its lively music and upbeat atmosphere.

**9 Cirrus 9**
The Oberoi Hotel's rooftop bar *(see p103)* offers guests well-curated music, a wide selection of cocktails and magnificent views.

**10 Aqua**
An elegant spot for drinks, Aqua *(see p82)* has an iridescent pool, curtained pavilions and designer bar.

**The alfresco bar at Aqua**

# 🔟 Bazaars of Old Delhi

### 1 Dariba Kalan
**MAP H3** ■ Chandni Chowk ■ Chandni Chowk Metro ■ Open 11am–8pm Mon–Sat

Dating back to the days of Emperor Shah Jahan, "The Street of the Incomparable Pearl" is Old Delhi's foremost jewellery bazaar. The shops here sell an array of precious stones and metals including an especially good selection of silverware, as well as traditional attar-based *itr* perfumes.

### 2 Ballimaran
**MAP G3** ■ Chandni Chowk ■ Chandni Chowk Metro ■ Open 11am–8pm Mon–Sat

The Chandni Chowk end of this long Old Delhi thoroughfare is the place to go to for shoes and slippers.

Dry fruits on sale at Khari Baoli

### 3 Khari Baoli
**MAP F3** ■ Chandni Chowk ■ Chandni Chowk Metro ■ Open 11am–8pm Mon–Sat

Said to be the biggest spice market in Asia, Khari Baoli is one of Old Delhi's most absorbing sights. Lively and congested in equal measure, it is lined with shops crammed full of all kinds of spices, pulses, dried fruits and other cooking ingredients.

The crowded stalls of Kinari Bazaar

### 4 Kinari Bazaar
**MAP G3** ■ Chandni Chowk ■ Chandni Chowk Metro ■ Open 11am–8pm Mon–Sat

Just off Dariba Kalan, the shops of Kinari Bazaar are famous for their wedding paraphernalia and other "fancy goods" – garlands of fake flowers and banknotes, reams of gold and silver tinsel, bridal veils, turbans for grooms, and sparkly costume jewellery. They also sell items used in the *Ramayana* performances that are staged all over the city during the festival of Dussehra.

### 5 Guliyan Bazaar
**MAP G4** ■ Chawri Bazaar Metro

Stretching around the northwestern side of Jama Masjid, this is the place to come to stock up on fireworks for a wedding or a festival, with shops filled with piles of brightly coloured boxes full of rockets, firecrackers and other things that go bang.

### 6 Nai Sarak
**MAP G4** ■ Chawri Bazaar Metro

This street, created by the British in 1857 (hence the name, meaning "New Street"), cuts across the heart of the old city. It is now Old Delhi's main book market, with small shops selling dog-eared, second-hand school and college textbooks.

### 7 Car Parts Bazaar
MAP G4 ■ Chawri Bazaar Metro

Sprawling around the south and west sides of the Jama Masjid, this is one of Old Delhi's more workaday bazaars selling mechanical bits and bobs. Visitors will find everything from wheels, doors, hubcaps, panels and entire engines – a surreal sight in the shadow of the beautiful mosque.

### 8 Katra Neel
MAP G3 ■ Chandni Chowk ■ Chandni Chowk Metro ■ Open 11am–8pm Mon–Sat

Just off Chandni Chowk, this fascinating labyrinth of tiny alleyways is cluttered with shops selling all manner of ladies' clothing – shawls, salwar kameezes, saris – and a wide variety of textiles, such as brocades from Benarasi, silk and voile.

### 9 Chawri Bazaar
MAP G4 ■ Chawri Bazaar Metro

Old Delhi's stationery bazaar is devoted to writing paper, greetings cards and other paper products. Paper here is sold by weight and is very cheap. Shops at the western end of the road specialize in lovely brass and copper ornaments.

### 10 Meena Bazaar
On the steps around the Jama Masjid is Old Delhi's religious bazaar (see p16), with stalls selling prayer rugs, Koranic inscriptions, pictures of Mecca and Islamic-style clocks.

**Prayer carpets at Meena Bazaar**

**TOP 10 SHOPS AND MARKETS**

Colourful handicrafts at Dilli Haat

**1 Dilli Haat**
A range of Indian craft items (see p96).

**2 State Emporia Complex**
MAP F7 ■ A–5 Baba Kharak Singh Marg
A must-visit for anyone interested in India's rich arts and crafts heritage.

**3 Janpath Market**
MAP F7 ■ Janpath ■ Open daily
Everything from export-reject clothes to pretty handmade paper lanterns.

**4 Khan Market**
MAP P5 ■ Open 10am–7:30pm Mon–Sat
Chic shops and restaurants, plus smaller shops selling lovely trinkets.

**5 Santushti**
Panchsheel Marg, Chanakyapuri ■ Open 10am–8pm daily
Classy shopping complex selling an assortment of beautiful designerwear.

**6 Connaught Place**
Elegant Georgian-style crescents housing Delhi's most important commercial space (see p77).

**7 Hauz Khas Village**
MAP U2 ■ Hauz Khas Village ■ Open 10am–8:30pm Mon–Sat
Lovely art galleries, cafés and shops.

**8 Sarojini Nagar**
MAP V1 ■ Sarojini Nagar ■ Open 10am–8:30pm Tue–Sun
Busy market selling clothes at low prices.

**9 Daryaganj Sunday Book Market**
MAP H5 ■ Open 7am–7pm Sun
A huge market for second-hand books, mostly in English.

**10 Select Citywalk Complex**
MAP V3 ■ A-3 District Centre Saket ■ 4211 4211 ■ Open 10am–11pm daily
Luxurious mall with stores offering major international brand names.

# ☰ Delhi for Free

**The fascinating ruins at Mehrauli Archaeological Park**

## 1 Mehrauli Archaeological Park

With over 70 monuments, including tombs, mosques, gateways and step-wells, from every century between the 13th and the 19th, this extensive park *(see p100)* is full of interesting sights and is also free to visit.

## 2 Films and Concerts

Alliance Française: 72 K K Birla Marg, Lodi Estate; https://delhi. afindia.org ■ American Center: 24 Kasturba Gandhi Marg; https://in. usembassy.gov

Cultural centres such as the American Center and the Alliance Française often host free movies, concerts and other events, although visitors may have to register or get passes in advance. The National Gandhi Museum *(see p54)* puts on free films about Gandhi's life (in English on Saturdays at 4pm).

## 3 Museums for Free

National Gallery of Modern Art: Guided walks at 11am, 1:30pm & 3:30pm

Not far from one another, the Indira Gandhi Memorial Museum *(see p78)*, the Pradhanmantri Sangrahalaya *(see p80)* and Gandhi Smriti *(see p79)* are all free. While there is an admission charge to enter the National Gallery of Modern Art *(see p80)*, the museum organises a series of guided walks, which take you around the exhibitions on display at no extra cost. Other free museums include the National Gandhi Museum *(see p54)*, the National Philatelic Museum *(see p54)* and the Sulabh International Museum of Toilets *(see p55)*.

## 4 Open-Air Gyms

Those looking for a free outdoor workout are in luck. The New Delhi Municipal Council has installed an array of fitness equipment in the Lodi Gardens *(see pp30–31)*, Nehru Park *(see p59)* and in a number of other parks across the city.

## 5 Change of Guard

MAP L3 ■ Gate No. 2 Rashtrapati Bhavan, Kartavya Path ■ Sat & Sun, check website for timings ■ www. rb.nic.in/rbvisit/visit_plan.aspx

Although visits to see the interior of the presidential palace *(see pp20–21)* incur a small booking fee, the weekly Change of Guard ceremony is free; just bring your passport.

**The Change of Guard ceremony**

### 6 Hindu temples

All Hindu temples are free to enter as long as you dress respectfully. The most popular are three modern temples – Lakshmi Narayan Mandir (see p79), Akshardham Temple (see p94) and Chhattarpur Mandir (see p61) – and the Gauri Shankar Mandir in Old Delhi (see p88).

### 7 Hauz Khas
**MAP U2 ■ Hauz Khas Village Road**

Alauddin Khilji's 14th-century Hauz-i-Alai reservoir (see p100) is free to visit, as is the nearby Deer Park (see p58). The road into the village from Aurobindo Marg has a string of 14th- and 15th-century tombs along it; these are also free to everyone.

### 8 Jahanpanah
**MAP W2 ■ Between the Outer Ring Road, Press Enclave Marg, Aurobindo Marg and Lal Bahadur Shastri Marg**

Delhi's fourth incarnation (see p51) is full of fascinating free sights, from the Begumpuri Masjid (see p100) and Bijay Mandal (see p61) to the Khirki Masjid (see p45) and Chiragh Delhi village (p101). Combined, they add up to a wonderful half-day walk.

### 9 Qawwalis in Nizamuddin

Anyone can attend the *dargah* at Nizamuddin (see p94) to hear *qawwalis*, the rhythmic chanting and singing used by devotees to achieve a trance-like state. Visitors should dress respectfully, as this is a religious shrine. It is also home to a cluster of Mughal monuments and the graves of various notable individuals, including poet and musician Amir Khusrau (1253–1325), Shah Jahan's daughter Jahanara and the great Urdu poet Mirza Ghalib (see p88).

### 10 Gurudwara Bangla Sahib

Delhi's biggest Sikh temple (see p52) offers free guided tours on request, with devotional music on tap, and a free meal of *dal* and *chapattis* three times daily for everyone.

**TOP 10 BUDGET TIPS**

**Auto-rickshaws in Old Delhi**

**1** For auto-rickshaws, use the pre-paid booths at Connaught Place, Janpath and transport terminals, paying an official set rate to avoid overcharging.

**2** The metro is much cheaper than a taxi or auto-rickshaw, and usually faster, with no haggling.

**3** You don't need to buy your holiday reading before your trip: bookshops in Delhi stock the latest bestsellers. There are also a number of second-hand booksellers (see p67) in the city.

**4** Most bars in Delhi have a happy hour early in the evening, typically with "buy one get one free" offers on Indian beers and spirits.

**5** A coffee at the Indian Coffee House (see p82) costs about a quarter of the price charged by other high-end espresso chains.

**6** Alternatively, drink tea: a nice, warming cup of *pukka chai* will cost around ₹10 on any street corner.

**7** Have a meal at a *dhaba* (local diner). If the food is freshly cooked, then hygiene shouldn't be an issue. If the menu isn't in English, it's a good idea to confirm the price before ordering.

**8** A couple of Delhi's best restaurants offer slightly less expensive set menus. At Bukhara (see p65), there's a lunchtime set menu, while Spice Route (see p64) has a tasting menu in the evening.

**9** It is possible to get a bespoke suit made by a tailor at Connaught Place, such as M Ram and Sons (see p81).

**10** A ticket for the Taj Mahal gives travellers a discounted rate for entry to Fatehpur Sikri and several sites around Agra if they go on the same day.

# TOP 10 Festivals and Events

**The Dare Devils stunt team at the Indian Republic Day Parade**

## 1 Republic Day Parade
**26 Jan**

India's biggest parade celebrates the inauguration of the Indian constitution on 26 January 1950. The parade begins at the foot of Raisina Hill (see p20) and ends at the Red Fort, with military march pasts, floats and a fly-past by the Indian Air Force. On 29 January, the Beating the Retreat ceremony at Vijay Chowk marks the end of the celebrations.

## 2 Surajkund Crafts Mela
**A fortnight in Feb**

Held in Surajkund, about 20 km (12 miles) south of Delhi, this is one of India's biggest craft fairs, showcasing works from all over the country in a lively carnivalesque atmosphere.

## 3 Vintage Car Rally
**Late Feb/Early Mar**

This car rally features around 100 vintage and postwar cars, with their owners dressed in period costume. The event attracts participants from all over the country.

**Surajkund Crafts Mela handicrafts**

## 4 National School of Drama Festivals
**May & Jun ▪ Adm**

Each year, the National School of Drama (see p62) hosts the Summer Theatre Festival, with classical and contemporary plays staged by the school's repertory company. In spring, it hosts the Bharat Rang Mahotsav, with plays by theatre companies from around the world.

## 5 International Mango Festival
**Late Jun/Early Jul**

Mango lovers can sample more than 500 different types of mango that are on offer at this annual celebration. The event is held at Talkatora Gardens (see p58) every year.

## 6 Phool Walon ki Sair
**Usually 3 days in Sep**

The colourful Festival of the Flower Sellers is held in Mehrauli (see p100) after the rainy season. The highlight is the procession of flower sellers, who carry ornate floral tributes to the shrine of Qutb Sahib (see p26). They are led by dancers and people playing the *shehnai*, a type of woodwind instrument.

###  The IIC Experience
Mid-Oct

Held at the IIC *(see p63)*, this festival of the arts hosts a wide range of cultural events from music and dance (both Indian and Western) to theatre, film and literature, and is accompanied by a good food festival.

### 8 Delhi Queer Pride Parade
Last Sun in Nov

The annual Delhi Queer Pride Parade, with around 12,000 participants, celebrates the LGBTQ+ community. The parade, which starts from Barakhamba Road, passes Tolstoy Marg before ending at Jantar Mantar.

### 9 Qutb Festival
Nov/Dec

A three-day music festival, with concerts held in the Qutb Minar Complex *(see pp24–5)*, ranging from soulful qawwali singers and virtuoso sitar players to young rock bands.

**A cosplayer at Delhi Comic Con**

### 10 Delhi Comic Con
Dec

Held over three days, this pop culture fest showcases the works of Indian and international comic artists. Similar to other comic cons held around the world, the Delhi edition also features comedy performances, panel discussions, and entertaining cosplay competitions.

---

### TOP 10 RELIGIOUS FESTIVALS

**A devotee with an idol of Ganesh**

**1 Maha Shivaratri**
**Late Feb/early Mar**
The "Great Night of Shiva" is marked with fasts and prayers.

**2 Holi**
**Mar**
Hindu spring festival where people douse each other with colour and water.

**3 Rama Navami**
**Late Mar/early Apr**
Celebration of the birth of Rama, with continuous readings of the *Ramayana*.

**4 Buddha Jayanti**
**May**
Festival celebrating the Buddha's birth, enlightenment and death.

**5 Krishna Janmashtami and Ganesh Chaturthi**
**Mid-Aug–mid-Sep**
Celebration of the birth of the Hindu gods Krishna and Ganesh.

**6 Dussehra**
**Mid-Sep–mid-Oct**
Ten-day celebration of the victory of good over evil, including Rama's over Ravana and Durga's over Mahishasura.

**7 Bakr Id**
**Sep/Oct**
The year's biggest Muslim festival, when the Jama Masjid area becomes a market for sacrificial goats.

**8 Diwali**
**Oct/Nov**
Five-day festival of lights honouring Rama's return to Ayodhya from exile.

**9 Guru Purab**
**All year**
Ten Sikh festivals, each celebrating the birth of one of the Sikh faith's ten gurus.

**10 Christmas**
**Dec**
Midnight mass is held in most churches on Christmas Eve.

# 🔟 Excursions from Delhi

**A monkey outside Mathura temple**

### 1 Mathura and Vrindavan
MAP C3

Mathura is reputed to be the birth place of the flute-playing Hindu deity, Krishna, while half a million pilgrims a year flock to the nearby town of Vrindavan and the hill of Govardhan, which Krishna is said to have lifted with just a single finger.

### 2 Amritsar
MAP B1

The holiest city of the Sikh faith is home to the Golden Temple, an unforgettable sight with the gilded Harmandir Sahib rising out of the surrounding lake.

### 3 Deeg
MAP B3 ■ Deeg Palace: open 9am–5pm Tue–Sun ■ Adm

This workaday town is home to one of the region's most spectacular palaces. Built in the 18th century by the local Jat rulers, the Deeg Palace blends Hindu and Mughal elements with spacious water gardens dotted with palaces and pavilions. The celebrated Keshav Bhawan (known as the Monsoon Palace) was designed to re-create the torrential rainfall and thunderous sounds of a wet-season downpour.

### 4 Sultanpur Bird Sanctuary
MAP B3 ■ 45 km (28 miles) SW of Delhi ■ Open 7am–4:30pm Wed–Mon ■ Adm and charge for video

About 45 km (28 miles) southwest of Delhi in Haryana state, the Sultanpur Bird Sanctuary makes for a peaceful rural outing. Centred on a large wetland area that fills up during the seasonal rains, the sanctuary attracts aquatic migratory birds and offers a number of walks through the serene woods.

**Kingfisher in Sultanpur Bird Sanctuary**

### 5 Keoladeo Ghana National Park
MAP C3 ■ Bharatpur district, 185 km (115 miles) E of Jaipur ■ Open Apr–Sep: 6am–6pm; Oct–Mar: 6:30am–5:30pm ■ Adm

This national park near the town of Bharatpur is one of India's finest birdwatching destinations. It is home to a huge number of resident and migratory species, including flocks of aquatic birds that come to nest in the park's wetlands.

### 6 Sariska Tiger Reserve

MAP B3 ■ Alwar district,
37 km (23 miles) SW of Alwar
■ Alwar tourist office: 0144 234
7348 ■ Open summer: 6–9am & 1–4pm
daily; winter: 7–10am & 2–5pm daily

An hour's drive beyond Alwar, the
Sariska Tiger Reserve was left with-
out any tigers in 2005, when it was
discovered that the park's entire
tiger population had vanished, pre-
sumably taken by poachers. With
a re-population programme, the
number of tigers is now believed
to be 14. The visitors can also see
a wide range of birdlife and a good
selection of Indian mammals, ranging from jackals to antelopes.

### 7 Fatehpur Sikri

MAP C3 ■ Open sunrise–
sunset daily ■ Adm

Around 40 km (25 miles) beyond
Agra lie the fascinating remains of
the ghost city of Fatehpur Sikri, built
by Akbar between 1569 and 1585,
but abandoned not long afterwards.
The city remains wonderfully
preserved, with superb red sandstone buildings and a magically
time-warped atmosphere.

### 8 Jaipur

MAP B3

Jaipur, the capital of Rajasthan, is a
fascinating city with many attractions,
ranging from the bazaars of the old
Pink City to the City Palace and the
Hawa Mahal, whose five-storey façade
is one of India's most famous sights.

### 9 Agra

Once capital of the entire
Mughal Empire, the large and
chaotic city of Agra is home to some
of India's most wonderful and
inspiring monuments, including the
impressive Agra Fort, the exquisite
Itimad-ud-Daulah, Emperor Akbar's
Tomb at Sikandra and, of course, the
magnificent Taj Mahal (see pp36–9).

**The city of Alwar in Rajasthan**

### 10 Alwar

MAP B3

Midway between Delhi and Jaipur,
the characterful little city of Alwar
is considered the traditional northern
gateway to Rajasthan. It features an
imposing fort with ramparts cresting
a series of hills above the town, and
an absorbing old city palace below.

**Ornate design of
Jaipur's Hawa Mahal**

# Delhi Area by Area

Humayun's Tomb, a stunning
example of Mughal architecture

| | |
|---|---|
| New Delhi | **76** |
| Old Delhi | **84** |
| South of the Centre | **92** |
| South Delhi | **98** |

# 📻 New Delhi

The city of New Delhi, built by the British between 1911 and 1931, still serves as the hub of Delhi's increasingly huge and formless urban expanse. The area is divided into two parts. The first is Connaught Place – a huge, vibrant circular plaza of Georgian crescents, that is home to shops, restaurants and other businesses, and is located at the commercial and residential heart of the city. The second, some 2 km (1 mile) south down Janpath, is the great Imperial thoroughfare of Kartavya Path, linking a triumphalist sequence of Raj-era landmarks, including India Gate and the Rashtrapati Bhavan. The area is also home to almost all the city's finest museums, plus a few relics dating back to the years before British rule.

**Sunga Dynasty sculpture, National Museum**

**Neo-Classical buildings at Connaught Place**

plaza occupies a pivotal position in the layout of the city, with roads radiating off in every direction. Colonnaded Neo-Classical buildings surround a central park, their shaded arcades hosting shops and restaurants.

## 1 Connaught Place (CP)
MAP F6 ■ Rajiv Chowk Metro
The commercial hub of New Delhi, Connaught Place, or CP (now officially rechristened Rajiv Chowk), was built between 1929 and 1933 to a design by British architect Robert Tor Russell. The enormous circular

## 2 National Museum
This is India's largest and most impressive museum *(see pp32–5)* with a vast collection of artifacts from prehistory to the 20th century. Highlights include a superb selection of ancient finds from the Indus Valley Civilization. Also on display is an array of wonderful Chola bronzes including a famous statuette of the dancing Shiva.

## 3 India Gate
At the eastern end of Kartavya Path *(see p20)* stands India Gate, built to commemorate the soldiers of the British Indian Army killed during World War I and the Afghan Wars. Beneath the arch burns an eternal flame in memory of soldiers who gave their lives in the 1971 Indo-Pakistan war. A statue of the freedom fighter Subhas Chandra Bose now stands under the red sandstone canopy. Beyond lies the National War Memorial, an obelisk topped by an eternal flame at the centre of four concentric circles.

| | |
|---|---|
| **1** | **Top 10 Sights** *see pp77–9* |
| **1** | **Places to Eat** *see p83* |
| **1** | **Places to Shop** *see p81* |
| **1** | **The Best of the Rest** *see p80* |
| **1** | **Bars and Cafés** *see p82* |

**Historic India Gate**

**Observatory at the Jantar Mantar**

### 4 Jantar Mantar

MAP F7 ▪ Sansad Marg ▪ Janpath Metro ▪ Open sunrise–sunset daily ▪ www.jantarmantar.org ▪ Adm

The Jantar Mantar was one of five outdoor astronomical observatories constructed by the Maharaja of Jaipur, Jai Singh II (the others are in Mathura, Jaipur, Varanasi and Ujjain). Built in 1724, it consists of four huge, strangely shaped stone instruments; these include the Samrat Yantra, a kind of monumental sundial centred on an enormous stone staircase, and the Misra Yantra, shaped like a huge inverted heart. The instruments were designed to perform various functions, including measuring exact solar and lunar calendars and tracking the movements of stars and accurate planetary positions.

### 5 Kartavya Path

Kartavya Path *(see pp20–21)* is the ceremonial axis of Lutyens' New Delhi and links most of the major landmarks of the "new city". It runs all the way from India Gate via Vijay Chowk up Raisina Hill, between the two Secretariat Buildings and on to Rashtrapati Bhavan. The main section, between India Gate and Vijay Chowk, forms Delhi's most impressive open space: a huge sprawling boulevard flanked by lawns, with dramatic views of the Imperial monuments in every direction.

### 6 Indira Gandhi Memorial Museum

MAP M5 ▪ 1 Safdarjung Road ▪ 2301 0094 ▪ Open 9:30am–5pm Tue–Sun

Formerly home to both Indira Gandhi and her son, Rajiv, this moving museum is also the site of Indira's assassination (1984) by two of her Sikh bodyguards. There is a wide-ranging array of displays on Indira's years in power, offering a glimpse into both her achievements and lapses into quasi-dictatorship, as well as an extensive collection of Rajiv's personal effects.

---

**CURSE OF THE CITY BUILDERS**

An old Persian prophecy claims that "Whoever builds a new city in Delhi will lose it". Several rulers of the city have experienced the force of this curse, but the most spectacular fall from grace was that of the British, who spent around 20 years building New Delhi, only to be forced out within 14 years of the city's completion.

---

### 7 Rashtrapati Bhavan

The centrepiece of New Delhi and generally regarded as Lutyens' masterpiece, the Rashtrapati Bhavan *(see p21)* is the residence of the President of India. It is India's finest example of colonial-era architecture. The work is a remarkable synthesis of Neo-Classical and Indian styles, exemplified by the huge dome, said to have been modelled partly on the Pantheon in Rome and partly on the Buddhist stupa at Sanchi.

**Exterior of Rashtrapati Bhavan**

### 8 Lakshmi Narayan Mandir

MAP D6 ■ Mandir Marg, near Connaught Place ■ R K Ashram Marg Metro ■ Open 4:30am–noon & 2–9pm daily ■ No cameras or mobile phones allowed

Built in 1938 by industrialist BD Birla, this temple is the biggest and most striking of the various shrines along Mandir Marg, with a clustered mass of red-and-orange *shikharas* (towers) centred on a large marble courtyard. Shrines to Durga and a meditating statue of Shiva stand within.

**Lakshmi Narayan Mandir**

### 9 National Crafts Museum

One of Delhi's most engaging and entertaining sights, this museum *(see pp28–9)* offers an alternative take on the nation's cultural heritage. In contrast to the classic artworks at the National Museum, the emphasis here is on local artisanal traditions, showcasing an incredibly varied – and often quirky – range of cultural, religious and architectural traditions from all over the subcontinent.

### 10 Gandhi Smriti

MAP N5 ■ 5 Tees January Marg ■ 2301 2843 ■ Open 10am–5pm Tue–Sun

It was here in 1948 that a Hindu fundamentalist assassinated Gandhi. The museum simultaneously serves as an absorbing exposition of Gandhi's life and work and also as a shrine to one of the 20th-century's most inspirational leaders. Stone footsteps mark the route of Gandhi's last walk.

## A DAY IN NEW DELHI

### ▶ MORNING

Begin your day exploring the varied exhibits at the engaging **National Crafts Museum** *(see pp28–9)*, then walk along to the eastern end of **Kartavya Path** and **India Gate** *(see p77)*. Continue on to the **National Museum** *(see p77)* and spend a couple more hours browsing its superb range of Indian artifacts. Stop for a snack at the museum's small café, or alternatively take an auto-rickshaw down to **Khan Market** *(see p67)*, which has a wide variety of restaurants and cafés from which to choose. Have lunch at SodaBottleOpenerWala *(see p97)* or Latitude 28 Café *(see p97)*.

### AFTERNOON

Continue walking west along the stately expanse of **Kartavya Path**, as Herbert Baker's Neo-Classical **Secretariat Buildings** *(see p80)* come gradually into view. Carry on to the top of Raisina Hill for a peek at Lutyens' masterpiece, **Rashtrapati Bhavan**; visits can be arranged by calling in advance *(see p21)*. From here, catch an auto-rickshaw, or walk north via **Sansad Bhavan** *(see p80)*, to the 18th-century outdoor astronomical park of **Jantar Mantar**. Take your time inspecting the intriguing planetary instruments here, then walk 100 metres (110 yards) north to **Connaught Place** *(see p77)*, the heart of commercial New Delhi. Finish the day with a snack at one of the area's many restaurants *(see p83)*, or a drink at the bars and cafés *(see p82)*.

# The Best of the Rest

### 1 Secretariat Buildings

MAP M3 ■ Raisina Hill

Herbert Baker's grandiose Secretariat Buildings, framing Raisina Hill, are two of the city's finest examples of epic Neo-Classical style.

**Crest, Secretariat Buildings**

### 2 Hanuman Mandir

MAP F7 ■ Baba Kharak Singh Marg ■ Open 5am–11pm daily

This temple has a richly decorated interior with ornate, gilded shrines.

### 3 Gurudwara Bangla Sahib

MAP E7 ■ Ashoka Road ■ Open daily

The Bangla Sahib is Delhi's most important Sikh *gurudwara* (temple).

### 4 Agrasen's Baoli

MAP G7 ■ Off Hailey Road, Kasturba Gandhi Marg ■ Open daily

This spectacularly deep *baoli* (stepwell), now dry, is thought to have been built by Raja Agrasen (or Ugrasen) in the 14th century.

**Agrasen's impressive *baoli***

### 5 Pradhanmantri Sangrahalaya

MAP L5 ■ Teen Murti Marg ■ 2141 0360 ■ Open 9am–5:30pm Tue–Sun ■ www.pmsangrahalaya.gov.in

The former home of India's first prime minister is now a museum dedicated to all prime ministers of India since independence.

### 6 National Gallery of Modern Art (NGMA)

MAP Q3 ■ Jaipur House ■ 2338 6111 ■ Open 11am–6pm Tue–Fri (to 8pm Sat & Sun) ■ www.ngmaindia.gov.in

This gallery has an outstanding range of colonial and modern Indian art.

### 7 National Philatelic Museum

MAP N2 ■ Dak Bhawan, Sardar Patel Chowk, Sansad Marg ■ 2303 6447 ■ Open 10am–5pm Mon–Fri

A philatelic paradise, with displays covering every stamp issued by India since independence, as well as some older, but well-preserved, exhibits.

### 8 Sansad Bhavan

MAP M2 ■ Lok Sabha Marg ■ Closed to the public

Designed by Lutyens, this edifice is home to the Indian parliament.

### 9 Cathedral Church of the Redemption

MAP L2 ■ 1 Church Road, North Avenue ■ Open 9am–6pm daily

This is Delhi's grandest Anglican church and one of the city's last major Raj-era buildings (1931).

### 10 St Martin's Church

MAP A6 ■ Off Cariappa Marg, near Dhaula Kuan and NH8

Built in 1930, this church is an intriguing British architectural venture. The sparse, fortress-like exterior makes it one of Delhi's most unusual churches.

# Places to Shop

**1** **The Shop**
MAP F6 ■ 10 Regal Building,
Connaught Place ■ 2334 0971
■ Open 9:30am–7:30pm Mon–Sat,
noon–7pm Sun

An array of Indian homewares and
lifestyle products is sold at this store.

The Shop, ideal for gifts

**2** **Bangle Market**
MAP F7 ■ Hanuman Mandir,
Baba Kharak Singh Marg, Connaught
Place ■ Open 11am–8pm daily

An open-air market next to Hanuman
Mandir, this place offers an amazing
variety of bangles from all over the
country. Avoid going on Tuesday as
the temple gets very crowded.

**3** **Central Cottage Industries Emporium**
MAP F7 ■ Jawahar Vyapar Bhavan,
Janpath ■ 2332 0554 ■ Open 10am–
7pm daily

This government initiative was set
up to preserve and develop handicrafts from all over the country.

**4** **Khadi India**
MAP F6 ■ Khadi Gramodyog
Bhavan, 24 Regal Building,
Connaught Place ■ 20513 8016
■ Open 11am–7pm daily

A government initiative, Khadi India
supports the production of Indian
fabrics, natural cosmetics, organic
food, pottery and handmade paper.

**5** **Tribes India**
MAP F7 ■ Gallery 2, Rajiv
Gandhi Handicrafts Bhavan, Baba
Kharak Singh Marg ■ 99584 53908
■ Open 10am–9pm Mon–Sat

A store that stocks some lovely tribal
handicrafts from all over the country.

**6** **Soma**
MAP F6 ■ K-44 Connaught
Place ■ 2341 2966 ■ Open 10am–
8pm daily

At Soma you can find dresses and
home furnishings, block-printed by
hand using a traditional Indian method.

**7** **Kamala**
MAP F7 ■ Gallery 1, Rajiv
Gandhi Handicrafts Bhavan, Baba
Kharak Singh Marg ■ 98991 08836
■ Open 10am–7pm Mon–Sat

Kamala is known for its handicrafts,
jewellery, folk paintings, pottery, and
handwoven and printed fabrics.

**8** **State Emporia Complex**
MAP F6 ■ Pallika Kendra,
Baba Kharak Singh Marg ■ Shivaji
Stadium Metro ■ Open 11am–
6:30pm Mon–Sat

Shop for a range of regional
merchandise including crafts,
paintings, saris, jewellery and
much more.

**9** **Rikhi Ram**
MAP F6 ■ G-8 Connaught
Place ■ 2332 7685 ■ Open 11am–
8pm Mon–Sat

Many musicians, such as the late Ravi
Shankar, have bought their sitars and
tablas from this long-established
firm, still crafting traditional musical
instruments the old-fashioned way.

**10** **M Ram and Sons**
MAP F6 ■ E-21 Connaught
Place ■ 2341 8364 ■ Open 10am–8pm
Mon–Sat (Sep–Feb: 11am–7pm Sun)

This tailoring firm has been in
business since 1939. They can make
a bespoke suit in no time at all, for a
fraction of department store prices.

*See map on pp76–7*

# Bars and Cafés

The stunning outdoor space, overlooking the pool, at Aqua

### 1 Aqua
MAP F7 ■ The Park, 15 Parliament Street ■ 2374 3000 ■ Open 11am–midnight daily

A glamorous alfresco bar and dining space, this place also has a pool and chic white-curtained pavilions.

### 2 Rick's
MAP P4 ■ The Taj Mahal Hotel, 1 Man Singh Road ■ 6651 3246 ■ Open 4pm–1am daily

Everyone's favourite in town, Rick's *(see p65)* is an understated and intimate bar with an extensive wine list.

### 3 1911
MAP F7 ■ The Imperial, 1 Janpath ■ 4111 6603 ■ Open 11:30–12:45am daily

Replete with old-world charm, 1911 is best enjoyed on a sunny afternoon over a chilled beer.

### 4 Triveni Tea Terrace
MAP Q1 ■ Triveni Kala Sangam, 205 Tansen Marg ■ 99715 66904 ■ Open noon–8pm daily

Sharing space with four art galleries, this is a charming spot for relaxing.

### 5 Cha Bar
MAP G7 ■ N-81 Barakhamba Road, Connaught Place ■ 99109 94865 ■ Open 11am–9:30pm daily

Housed in the Oxford Bookstore, the Cha Bar offers an extensive tea list.

### 6 Indian Coffee House (ICH)
MAP F7 ■ 2nd floor, Mohan Singh Place Shopping Complex, Baba Kharak Singh Marg, off Connaught Place ■ 2334 2994 ■ Open 9am–9pm daily

The venerable ICH serves excellent south Indian coffee at low prices.

### 7 Q'BA
MAP F6 ■ E-42/43 Connaught Place ■ 4517 3333 ■ Open noon–1am daily

The terrace has fairy lights and an excellent view of Connaught Place.

### 8 Agni
MAP F7 ■ The Park, 15 Parliament Street ■ 2374 3000 ■ Open 5pm–12:30am, days vary, call ahead

Loud and fun, Agni is a great place for *bhangra* (Punjabi dance).

### 9 Ministry of Beer
MAP G6 ■ M-44, Outer Circle, Connaught Place ■ 88000 12060 ■ Open noon–1am daily

Head to Ministry of Beer to unwind and sample the wide selection of beer and quirky cocktails on offer.

### 10 Kitty Su
MAP G6 ■ Lalit Hotel, Tolstoy Marg, off Barakhamba Road ■ 99586 56622 ■ Open 10pm–1am Tue–Sun

There is mainly electronic music at this vibrant hotel nightclub with DJs, regular concerts and parties.

# Places to Eat

**PRICE CATEGORIES**

For a meal for one, inclusive of taxes and service charge but not alcohol.

₹ under ₹500 ₹₹ ₹500–1,500
₹₹₹ over ₹1,500

##  House of Ming

MAP P4 ■ The Taj Mahal Hotel, 1 Man Singh Road ■ 6651 3242 ■ Open 12:30–2:45pm & 7:30–11:45pm daily ■ ₹₹₹

This swanky restaurant *(see p65)* serves excellent Chinese food.

## 2 Andhra Bhawan

MAP P2 ■ 1 Ashoka Road ■ 2338 7499 ■ Open 8–10:30am, noon–3:30pm & 7:30–10pm daily ■ ₹

The finest spicy Andhra food, served at extremely reasonable prices.

## 3 Spice Route

MAP F7 ■ The Imperial, 1 Janpath ■ 4111 6605 ■ Open 12:30–2:45pm & 7–11:45pm daily ■ ₹₹₹

Fine cuisine inspired by places along the Spice Route *(see p64)*.

## 4 Veda

MAP F6 ■ H-26 Connaught Place ■ 90299 02950 ■ Open noon–11:30pm daily ■ ₹₹

An opulent restaurant that serves top-notch food – from the *murgh malai tikka* to Parsi sea bass.

## 5 Rajdhani

MAP F6 ■ 9-A Atmaram Mansion, Scindia House, Connaught Place ■ 4350 1200 ■ Open noon–3:30pm & 7–11pm daily ■ ₹₹

Rajdhani is known for its Gujarati food. It serves a delectable vegetarian thali.

## 6 Pindi

MAP P4 ■ 16 Pandara Road Market ■ 2338 7932 ■ Open noon–midnight daily ■ ₹₹

This legendary restaurant dates back to 1948 and is famous for its tandoori specialities and seafood.

## 7 Fire

MAP F7 ■ The Park, 15 Parliament Street ■ 84481 46709 ■ Open noon–3pm & 6–11pm daily ■ ₹₹₹

A smart, contemporary restaurant serving fine modern Indian cuisine, with a seasonal menu, light in summer, fiery hot in winter.

## 8 Daniell's Tavern

MAP F7 ■ The Imperial, 1 Janpath ■ 4111 6607 ■ Open 6:30–11:45pm daily ■ ₹₹₹

This elegant spot is inspired by the travels of the late 18th-century artists Thomas and William Daniell, and serves plates of first-rate Indian cuisine.

## 9 Varq

MAP P4 ■ The Taj Mahal Hotel, 1 Man Singh Road ■ 6651 3151 ■ Open 12:30–2:45pm & 7–11:45pm daily ■ ₹₹₹

A stylish, relaxed restaurant, Varq serves truly delicious Indian food. Try the lamb cooked in a saffron crust or the excellent crispy Calicut prawns.

**Elegant interior of Varq**

## 10 Saravana Bhavan

MAP F7 ■ 50 Janpath ■ 2331 7755 ■ Open 8am–11pm daily ■ ₹

When it comes to south Indian food in Delhi, Saravana Bhavan *(see p64)* is the place to go. Get the mini-tiffin to sample a variety of dishes.

*See map on pp76–7*

# TOP 10 Old Delhi

The city of Shahjahanabad was originally built by Mughal emperor Shah Jahan between 1638 to 1648 to replace the previous Mughal capital of Agra. Now generally known as Old Delhi, it is the most rewarding part of the city. This is Delhi at its most traditional and atmospheric: a fascinating labyrinth of tiny alleyways, colourful bazaars and a profusion of historical monuments and religious shrines, including two of Delhi's landmark attractions: the magnificent Red Fort and the grand Jama Masjid. There are further – albeit more modest – points of interest north of Old Delhi in the quiet Civil Lines district, where the British first established themselves in the city, and along the lush Northern Ridge, where they sought refuge during the opening months of the 1857 Uprising.

**Shakti Sthal, Raj Ghat**

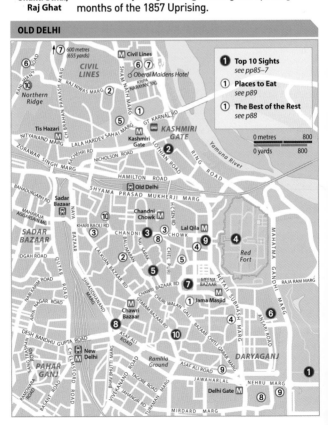

**OLD DELHI**

Top 10 Sights
see pp85–7

Places to Eat
see p89

The Best of the Rest
see p88

### 1 Raj Ghat
MAP J5 ▪ Mahatma Gandhi Marg ▪ Delhi Gate Metro ▪ Open sunrise–sunset daily

Dedicated to Mahatma Gandhi, this austere memorial features an open, black marble platform surrounded by a white marble fence. Gandhi's last words, "Hey Ram" ("Oh God"), are inscribed on the platform where his funeral rites were performed. Set back from the banks of the Yamuna, Raj Ghat is surrounded by landscaped gardens. Trees planted by visiting dignitaries have been identified using plaques. Nearby stand memorials to other national leaders including Shanti Vana (Jawaharlal Nehru) and Shakti Sthal (Indira Gandhi).

### 2 St James' Church
MAP G2 ▪ Lothian Road ▪ Kashmiri Gate Metro ▪ Open 9:30am–12:45pm & 2:30–4:30pm daily

This 19th-century architectural gem was built by Colonel James Skinner in 1836 – a perfect period piece, constructed in an unusual cruci-form pattern with a large dome over the central crossing. In and around the church stand memorials to some of the city's most colourful early British residents, including William Fraser, Thomas Metcalfe (see p27) and Colonel James Skinner.

### 3 Chandni Chowk
Old Delhi's main thoroughfare, and one of the most colourful streets in Delhi, Chandni Chowk (see pp14–15)

**A market stall at Chandni Chowk**

runs dead straight from the gates of the Red Fort due west to the Fatehpuri Masjid (see p15), passing a range of shops and shrines en route. The road's name, meaning Moonlit Square, is said to refer to a square that once stood about halfway along the road, and which was known for the moon-lit reflections in the canal that ran through its centre.

### 4 Red Fort
The enormous Red Fort (see pp12–13) served as the residence of the Mughal emperors from its com-pletion in 1648 through to the 1857 Uprising, when the last emperor, Bahadur Shah Zafar II, was exiled to Burma and the British took over the fort, demolishing many of its buildings. What is left now is only a shadow of the original complex, but the surviving pavilions and gardens still give a sense of the sophisticated lifestyles of India's most powerful and cultured rulers.

**The impressive Red Fort**

### 5 Bazaars of Old Delhi

Although much of the physical fabric of Old Delhi is fairly modern – due to damage sustained during the 1857 Uprising and 20th-century rebuilding – the entire area retains its original, labyrinthine street plan and much of its traditional atmosphere. Different areas have bazaars (see pp66–7) devoted to different trades and crafts – from jewellery and wedding gifts to fireworks and even some spare car parts.

**Colourful Kinari Bazaar in Old Delhi**

### 6 Zinat ul Masjid

MAP J4 ■ Ghata Masjid Road, Daryaganj ■ Taxi or rickshaw ■ Open sunrise–sunset daily

Hidden away in the streets of Daryaganj, this lovely mosque was commissioned in 1707 by Zinat ul Nisa, Aurangzeb's daughter, and is popularly known as the Ghata Masjid. Zinat ul Nisa was buried here in 1711, but her tomb was apparently removed by the British after the Uprising, when the mosque was taken over for military use.

### 7 Jama Masjid

The Jama Masjid (see pp16–17) is unquestionably the most beautiful of Old Delhi's Mughal monuments, looming high above the surrounding streets on a natural hillock and dominating all views of the old city. The approach from Meena Bazaar up to the eastern gate, facing the Red Fort, is particularly dramatic, although visitors now have to enter via the rather less imposing gateway on the western side.

### 8 Ajmeri Gate

MAP G4 ■ Ajmeri Gate Road ■ Chawri Bazaar Metro

Marooned on a small island amidst busy traffic, this is perhaps the most impressive of the four surviving gateways that once punctuated the old city walls. The fine old *madrasa* and Mosque of Ghazi-ud-Din, built in classic Mughal style, stand just opposite. Elsewhere in the old city, the Delhi, Kashmiri and Turkman gates also survive in good condition – the last is named after the revered Sufi saint, Hazrat Shah Turkman.

**Ornate onion domes and arches at the Zinat ul Masjid mosque**

The iconic Lal Mandir temple

## ⑨ Lal Mandir

Delhi's most important Jain temple, Lal Mandir *(see p14)* is located directly opposite the Red Fort, at the southern end of Chandni Chowk. Founded during the rule of Shah Jahan, the present building dates from the 1870s. The colourful interior is adorned with dozens of diminutive statues of various Jain *tirthankaras*. The temple's well-known bird hospital stands next door, caring for hundreds of hungry and injured pigeons and other birds, in tiny cages.

### HAZRAT SHAH TURKMAN

Delhi's Turkman Gate is named after a *bayabani* ("jungle dwelling") Sufi hermit, Hazrat Shah Turkman (d 1240), who lived nearby when the area was still forest. Despite his seclusion, his fame as a holy man spread, and many sought him out. His tiny *dargah* (tomb and mosque) is hidden away in the back alleys. Razia Sultan, a devoted follower of his, was buried nearby.

## ⑩ Tomb of Razia Sultan

MAP G4 ▪ Off Sitaram Bazaar Road ▪ Chawri Bazaar Metro ▪ Open sunrise–sunset daily

The tomb is in a roofless enclosure that was built here long before the city that surrounds it for its proximity to Turkman's tomb. The only female monarch until Queen Victoria to rule a vast swathe of the subcontinent, Razia was loved by the people but hated by the aristocracy, who resented having a woman as their ruler and overthrew her after a four-year reign.

### A DAY IN OLD DELHI

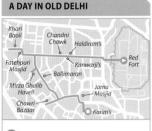

▶ **MORNING**

Start your day at the **Red Fort** *(see p85)* – arrive early to avoid the crowds. Spend a couple of hours exploring the complex; stop at the food stall outside the main gate for a quick bite. Exit the fort and walk up **Chandni Chowk** *(see p85)*, stopping by the various attractions en route. Stop at **Haldiram's** *(see p89)*, halfway up the road, for a tasty Indian fast-food lunch, then cross the road to **Kanwarji's**, established in 1850 and Delhi's oldest sweet shop since the closure of the famed Ghantewala's, founded in 1790 and once purveyor of sweets to the Mughal emperors.

**AFTERNOON**

Carry on up Chandni Chowk to the **Fatehpuri Masjid** *(see p15)*, then on to the remarkable spice market of **Khari Baoli** *(see p66)*, just beyond. From here, you can either retrace your steps down Chandni Chowk, then turn right down Dariba Kalan, or alternatively head down **Ballimaran** *(see p66)* to visit the *haveli* of the great Urdu poet **Mirza Ghalib** *(see p88)* and then **Chawri Bazaar**, through the heart of Old Delhi's bazaars. Much of the fun lies in simply wandering at will; aim to get lost at least once. Whichever route you take, be at the **Jama Masjid** towards sunset, when this superb mosque is at its most memorable, and the views over the old city and Red Fort are at their best. On leaving the mosque, you will be within a few steps of **Karim's** *(see p89)*, one of Old Delhi's culinary institutions and a perfect spot for an early dinner.

*See map on p84* ←

# The Best of the Rest

## 1 Qudsia Bagh

MAP G1 ■ Lala Hardev Sahai Marg ■ Open sunrise–sunset daily

Just north of the old city, these lovely, peaceful wooded gardens are home to a couple of fine buildings dating back to the gardens' foundation during the 18th century.

Qudsia Bagh

## 2 Mirza Ghalib Haveli

MAP G3 ■ Qasimjan Gali, off Ballimaran ■ Open 10am–6pm Tue–Sun

The former home of the great Urdu poet Mirza Ghalib (1797–1869) has been carefully restored and is now a simple museum, with a few exhibits on the writer's life and times.

## 3 Hauzwali Mosque

MAP G5 ■ Chandni Chowk ■ Chandni Chowk Metro ■ Open sunrise–sunset daily

This little blue mosque is one of the few surviving buildings from the time of Suri ruler Sher Khan.

## 4 Gauri Shankar Mandir

MAP H3 ■ Chandni Chowk

One of Old Delhi's largest and most popular Hindu temples, Gauri Shankar Mandir *(see p15)* is dedicated to Shiva (Shankar) and Parvati (Gauri).

## 5 Nicholson's Cemetery

MAP G1 ■ Lala Hardev Sahai Marg ■ Open daily

This beautiful, quiet colonial-era cemetery has the grave of Brigadier-General John Nicholson, who led the British assault on Delhi in 1857.

## 6 Pir Ghaib

MAP F1 ■ Hindu Rao Hospital Complex, Civil Lines ■ Open daily

Rising up north of Old Delhi is the long, forested Northern Ridge, dotted with British and Tughlaq monuments, such as the ruins of Pir Ghaib, a hunting lodge built by Feroz Shah Tughlaq in the 14th century.

## 7 Chauburji Masjid

MAP B4 ■ Chauburja Marg, Kamala Nehru Ridge, Tis Hazari ■ Open sunrise–sunset daily

A Tughlaq-era ruins in the Northern Ridge, this structure was built as a tomb around 1345, and subsequently converted into a mosque.

## 8 Feroz Shah Kotla

MAP J6 ■ Bahadur Shah Zafar Marg ■ Delhi Gate Metro ■ Open sunrise–sunset daily

All that remains of Sultan Feroz Shah Tughlaq's erstwhile citadel – now popularly thought to be the abode of djinns (spirits).

## 9 National Gandhi Museum

MAP J5 ■ Raj Ghat ■ 2331 0168 ■ Open 9:30am–5:30pm Tue–Sun ■ www.gandhimuseum.org

At the southern end of the Raj Ghat gardens, this museum offers personal insights into the Mahatma's life and works.

## 10 Ashoka Column

MAP E1 ■ Rani Jhansi Road ■ Pul Bangash Metro ■ Open daily

At the southern end of the Nothern Ridge is one of the city's two Ashokan columns *(see p51)*, from the reign of Ashoka (r 269–232 BCE).

Ashoka Column

See map on p84

# Places to Eat

**PRICE CATEGORIES**

For a meal for one, inclusive of taxes and
service charge but not alcohol.

₹ under ₹500  ₹₹ ₹500–1,500
₹₹₹ over ₹1,500

### 1 Karim's
MAP H4 ■ 16 Gali Kababiyan,
Matia Mahal, Jama Masjid ■ 2326
4981 ■ Open 9am–12:45pm daily ■ ₹

This *(see p65)* Delhi institution has
been serving delectable Mughlai
food for over half a century.

### 2 Gujarati Samaj Santushti
MAP F1 ■ 2 Raj Niwas
Marg, Civil Lines ■ 2398 1796
■ Open 6–10am, 11:30am–3pm
& 7–10pm daily ■ ₹

Tuck into tasty Gujarati food at this
government-run canteen.

### 3 Haldiram's
MAP G3 ■ 1454/2 Chandni
Chowk ■ 4768 5219 ■ Open
9am–10:30pm daily ■ ₹

The menu at Haldiram's consists of
hygienically prepared Indian street
food items and sweets.

### 4 Moti Mahal
MAP H5 ■ 3703 Netaji Subhash
Marg, Daryaganj ■ 4245 8399 ■ Open
11am–12:30am daily ■ ₹₹

This restaurant claims to have
invented the famous butter chicken.

### 5 Lakhori
2293, Gali Guliyan, Chandni
Chowk ■ 4909 1777 ■ Open 6:30am–
10:30pm (booking essential) ■ ₹₹₹

Lakhori takes its name from the red
kiln-baked bricks which make up its
interior and serves Mughlai cuisine.

### 6 The Curzon Room
MAP G1 ■ Oberoi Maidens,
7 Sham Nath Marg, Civil Lines ■ 2397
5464 ■ Open 7–11pm daily (buffet:
7:30–10pm) ■ ₹₹₹

Dig into the sumptuous buffet at this
elegant Raj-style restaurant.

### 7 The Garden Terrace
MAP G1 ■ Oberoi Maidens,
7 Sham Nath Marg, Civil Lines
■ 2397 5464 ■ Open daily 7am–
11pm ■ ₹₹

Spilling into a lovely courtyard,
The Garden Terrace, part of the
venerable Maidens Hotel, is an ideal
place for nursing a cup of coffee.

### 8 Paranthe Wali Gali
MAP G3 ■ Opposite Natraj
Restaurant, 1396 Chandni Chowk
■ Open 11am–11pm daily ■ ₹

The "alley of parantha-makers"
is a real foodie's delight, offering
an overwhelming variety of this
delicious stuffed Indian bread.

**Old-style charm at Chor Bizarre**

### 9 Chor Bizarre
MAP H5 ■ Hotel Broadway,
4/15A Asaf Ali Road ■ 4366 3600
■ Open noon–3pm & 7:30–11pm
daily ■ ₹₹

One of the oldest restaurants in Old
Delhi, Chor Bizarre *(see p64)* is famous
for its superb Kashmiri cuisine.

### 10 Kake di Hatti
MAP G3 ■ 654 Church
Mission Road, Fatehpuri, Chandni
Chowk ■ 98109 09754 ■ Open
8am–1am daily ■ ₹

This place draws flocks of locals to
mop up its legendary *daal makhni*.

*Following pages* The Diwan-i-Aam audience hall at Delhi's Red Fort

# TOP10 South of the Centre

The area south of New Delhi, now home to some of the city's most upmarket suburbs, features a superb swathe of Mughal (and some Sultanate) monuments. At the top of most visitors' lists is the magnificent Humayun's Tomb, the first great masterpiece of Mughal architecture, though there are also stand-out attractions nearby at the wonderfully atmospheric religious enclave of Nizamuddin, the beautiful parklands and historic monuments of the Lodi Gardens, Safdarjung's Tomb, and the rugged citadel of Purana Qila, while just across the Yamuna River lies Akshardham Temple, India's most extravagant modern Hindu shrine.

**Khan-i-Khanan's Tomb**

### 1 Khan-i-Khanan's Tomb
MAP R7 ■ Mathura Road, south of Humayun's Tomb ■ JLN Metro ■ Open sunrise–sunset daily ■ Adm

This grandiose tomb is the burial place of Abdur Rahim, Akbar's prime minister, who died in 1626, although it may have been built for his wife, who died in 1598. The tomb has four grand *iwans* and a bulbous central dome surrounded by *chhatris*, rather like a sketch for the Taj Mahal minus the minarets.

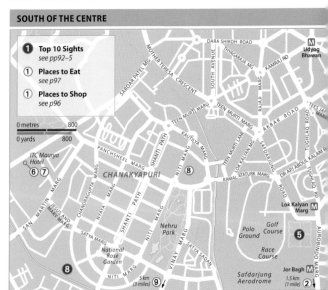

### SOUTH OF THE CENTRE

**1** Top 10 Sights
see pp92–5

**1** Places to Eat
see p97

**1** Places to Shop
see p96

0 metres    800
0 yards    800

ITC Maurya Hotel
**6** **7**

CHANAKYAPURI **8**

Nehru Park

National Rose Garden

**8**

Udyog Bhawan M

Lok Kalyan Marg M

Polo Ground

Golf Course

**5**

Race Course

Safdarjung Aerodrome

Jor Bagh

1.5 km (1 mile) **2**

5 km (3 miles) **9**

### 2 Purana Qila

MAP R3 ■ Mathura Road ■ Pragati Maidan Metro ■ Open sunrise–sunset daily ■ Adm

The sixth city of Delhi, the Purana Qila *(see p51)* was begun by Humayun and completed by his rival Sher Shah Suri. Its large, rugged walls stretch for over a mile and enclose a large swathe of parkland dotted with buildings. The most notable are the striking Qala-i-Kuhna Masjid, and the more delicate Sher Mandal, an unusual octagonal pavilion that was used by Humayun as a library and observatory.

**A baby hippo at the Zoological Park**

### 3 National Zoological Park

MAP R4 ■ Mathura Road, near Purana Qila ■ Pragati Maidan Metro ■ Open Apr–Oct: 9am–4:30pm Sat–Thu; Nov–Mar: 9am–4pm Sat–Thu; closed Fri ■ Adm ■ www.nzp newdelhi.gov.in

The largest of its kind in India, Delhi's popular zoo is home to around 2,000 animals, including national treasures such as rhinos, elephants and Bengal tigers, and a good selection of wildlife from the Americas, Australia and Africa.

Spread out over expansive parkland, it provides a pleasant, sympathetic environment for animals, as well as a peaceful refuge for the city's human population. It is also a great spot for a weekend picnic.

### 4 Lodi Gardens

The beautiful Lodi Gardens *(see pp30–31)* are among Delhi's most attractive retreats, offering a beguiling combination of nature and culture, with an idyllic wooded landscape dotted with fine tombs dating from the Lodi and Sayyid dynasties.

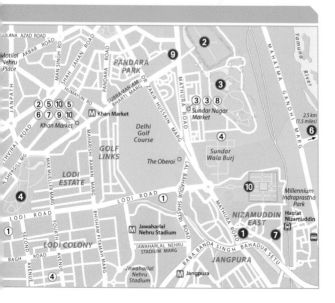

Safdarjung's Tomb, set in a *charbagh*-style garden

### (5) Safdarjung's Tomb

**MAP M6 ■ Airforce Golf Course, at the intersection of Safdarjung Road & Aurobindo Marg ■ Jor Bagh Metro ■ Open sunrise–sunset daily ■ Adm**

This mausoleum was built in 1754 for Safdarjung (1708–54), the Nawab of Awadh and one of the most important Mughal nobles during the reigns of Muhammad Shah and Ahmad Shah Bahadur. A good example of late-Mughal design, the tomb is a large and floridly decorated sandstone structure with a bulbous dome set in a *charbagh*-style garden.

#### LAST RITES, DELHI-STYLE

No other city in the world has as copious a range of mausoleums as Delhi – from certain angles the city can look like a kind of enormous necropolis. Oddly enough, such buildings run directly contrary to Koranic orthodoxy, which forbids the construction of elaborate funerary monuments – a prohibition that was ignored by the city's rulers.

### (6) Akshardham Temple

**MAP C5 ■ Taxi or Akshardham Metro ■ Open 9:30am–6:30pm Tue–Sun ■ Electronic equipment not allowed ■ www.akshardham.com**

Opened in 2005, this is perhaps the largest and most spectacular modern Hindu temple in India. The huge complex is centred on an extravagant shrine, ringed by 148 elephant statues; inside is an impressive-looking golden figure of Bhagwan Shri Swaminarayan, in whose honour the temple was built. The temple hosts exhibitions and even has a fountain water show at sunset.

### (7) Nizamuddin Dargah

**MAP R6 ■ Taxi or Hazrat Nizamuddin Metro ■ Open 24 hrs ■ Hope Project reservations: 2435 7081 ■ Qawwali: 98117 78607; 9–10pm Thu ■ www.nizamuddin aulia.org**

This atmospheric religious enclave grew up around the tomb of the great Sufi saint Hazrat Nizamuddin Auliya (1238–1325), and is quite busy with pilgrims at all hours, with performances of devotional

Shop outside Nizamuddin Dargah

*qawwali* singing held after dark. Hope Project, a local NGO, organizes evening walking tours of the adjoining Nizamuddin village, which are a fascinating way to learn about this area.

### 8 National Rail Museum

MAP U1 ■ Service Road, Chanakyapuri ■ Dhaula Kuan Metro ■ 2688 1826 ■ Open 10am–5pm Tue–Sun ■ Adm and charge for video and train rides

The National Rail Museum is a shrine to India's fascination with all things pertaining to the train. Among the highlights are the lavish carriages of local and foreign royals, including the Prince of Wales and the Maharaja of Mysore.

**Locomotive, National Rail Museum**

### 9 Khair ul Manazil Masjid

MAP Q4 ■ Mathura Road, opposite Purana Qila ■ Pragati Maidan Metro ■ Open sunrise–sunset daily

Just across the road from the Purana Qila lies the impressive, though now rather derelict, Khair ul Manazil Masjid, built in 1562 by Maham Anga, the powerful wet-nurse of Akbar. The mosque is a classic example of early Mughal architecture, its low and rather stocky façade reminiscent of the earlier Sultantate style.

### 10 Humayun's Tomb

One of the greatest of all Mughal garden tombs, this superb mausoleum *(see pp18–19)* is one of Delhi's finest monuments and a magnificent memorial to the personable but erratic Humayun, the second Mughal emperor.

### A DAY SOUTH OF THE CENTRE OF DELHI

▶ **MORNING**

It is possible to see most of the major sights covered in this section in one long, albeit very busy, day. Note that you will need taxis or auto-rickshaws to get to these places. Alternatively, hire one for the day. The highlights of the **Akshardham** temple can be seen in two hours, but for a more leisurely visit, allow half a day. Alternatively, you could pick from the following selection for a more relaxed tour.

Start your day at the imposing **Safdarjung's Tomb**, then walk a short distance down the road to the **Lodi Gardens** *(see p93)*. Explore the various tombs that dot the beautiful parkland – don't miss the lovely bonsai garden. Relax and have lunch at the classy **Perch** *(see p97)* in nearby Khan Market *(see p67)*.

**AFTERNOON**

Take an auto-rickshaw to the magnificent **Purana Qila** *(see p93)*, then cross the road to visit the **Khair ul Manazil Masjid**. From here, you can get another auto-rickshaw down to **Humayun's Tomb** *(see p18)*. Explore the tomb and gardens and the other mausoleums that dot the vast complex, then walk across the road to the wonderful little *dargah* at **Nizamuddin**. For dinner, you could head to the nearby **Fabcafé by the Lake** *(see p97)* in Sunder Nursery, before or after attending the evening qawwali session at the *dargah*.

*See map on pp92–3* ←

# Places to Shop

###  1 The Bookshop
MAP N7 ■ 13/7 Main Market, Jor Bagh ■ 2469 7102

The Bookshop is lovingly stocked with a wide range of reading matter, from well-thumbed classics to pristine new arrivals.

### 2 Dilli Haat
MAP V1 ■ Opposite INA Market ■ 2611 9055 ■ Adm

A daily open-air market run by Delhi Tourism, with several stalls selling wonderful arts, crafts and food – from every single state in India.

### 3 Bharany's
MAP R4 ■ 14 Sundar Nagar Market ■ 2435 8528

Bharany's takes pride in every one of its handcrafted jewellery items. It also has a fine collection of textiles.

### 4 Mittal Tea House
MAP P7 ■ Shop 8, Lodi Colony Market ■ 96676 99111

The pleasant Mittal Tea House stocks beautifully packed Darjeeling, Assam and Nilgiri teas, as well as Kangra and Kashmiri green teas.

### 5 Good Earth
MAP P5 ■ 9-ABC Khan Market ■ 2464 7175

This luxurious store stocks a range of exclusively designed dining products, high-quality linen and some lovely home-decor items.

**Amrapali bracelet**

### 6 Silverline
MAP P5 ■ 7-A Khan Market ■ 2464 3017

The walls of this shop are lined with jewellery in antique and contemporary designs.

### 7 Amrapali
MAP P5 ■ 39 Khan Market ■ 4175 2024

The exclusive collection here includes exquisite contemporary jewellery, designer, enamel, traditional and antique pieces.

### 8 Ladakh Art Gallery
MAP R4 ■ 10 Sundar Nagar Market ■ 2435 5424

A lovely shop that specializes in beautiful Indian handcrafted jewellery in gold and silver.

### 9 Ogaan
MAP P5 ■ 77 Khan Market ■ 4175 7220

This shop has a splendid ensemble of clothes, accessories and jewellery by various Indian designers. It also provides a platform for Indian design and stocks some luxurious clothes that are exquisite in cut and design.

### 10 Anokhi
MAP P5 ■ 32 Khan Market ■ 2460 3423

Specializing in contemporary crafted textiles with roots in Jaipur, Anokhi stocks traditional and western wear.

**Good Earth, Khan Market**

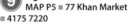

# Places to Eat

**PRICE CATEGORIES**
For a meal for one, including taxes and
service charge but not alcohol.

₹ under ₹500  ₹₹ ₹500–1,500
₹₹₹ over ₹1,500

### 1 Indian Accent
MAP Q6 ■ The Lodhi,
Lodi Road ■ 6617 5151 ■ Open
noon–3:30pm, 7–9:30pm &
9:45pm–12:45am daily ■ ₹₹₹

A swanky yet cosy venue *(see p64)* that
offers finely prepared local dishes.

### 2 Perch Wine & Coffee Bar
MAP P5 ■ 71, 1st Floor, Khan
Market ■ 83739 76637 ■ Open
8am–1am daily ■ ₹₹₹

A sophisticated coffee and wine
bar with great European cuisine.
The coffee sangria is a must try.

### 3 Diggin
MAP V2 ■ No. 1 & 2, Siri
Fort Marg ■ 4080 0081 ■ Open
11am–11pm daily ■ ₹₹

Comfy and quiet, Diggin *(see p65)*
is ideal for enjoying continental
meals on a lazy afternoon.

### 4 Fabcafe by the Lake
MAP H11 ■ Sunder Nursery
■ 74288 99692 ■ Open 7am–10pm
daily ■ ₹₹

Enjoy the wonderful location, casual
vibe and tasty, wholesome food at
this lovely café.

### 5 Latitude 28°
MAP P5 ■ Good Earth,
Khan Market ■ 2462 1013 ■ Open
11:30am–11:30pm daily ■ ₹₹₹

A stylish café that focuses on great
contemporary dishes with a twist.

### 6 Bukhara
MAP K5 ■ ITC Maurya, Sardar
Patel Marg ■ 2611 2233 ■ Open 12:30–
2:45pm & 7–11:45pm daily ■ ₹₹₹

This is one of the world's top Indian
restaurants *(see p65)*, serving superb
North-West Frontier cuisine.

**Dum Pukht's glamorous dining room**

### 7 Dum Pukht
MAP K5 ■ ITC Maurya, Sardar
Patel Marg ■ 2611 2233 ■ Open 12:30–
2:45pm & 7–11:45pm daily ■ ₹₹₹

Slow-cooked *dum* (steam casserole)
dishes from Lucknow, served amidst
tastefully glitzy surroundings.

### 8 Sagar Ratna
MAP L6 ■ The Ashok,
50-B Chanakyapuri ■ 2688 8242
■ Open 8am–11pm daily ■ ₹

Famous for its enormous *dosas*,
Sagar Ratna is an excellent place for
south Indian meals. Try the *thali* and
the south Indian filter coffee.

### 9 Coast Café
MAP U2 ■ H-2, Hauz Khas
Village ■ 4160 1717 ■ Open
noon–1am daily ■ ₹₹

This restaurant serves curries from
coastal Kerala, fish and chicken
stews as well as delicious cocktails.

### 10 SodaBottleOpenerWala
MAP P5 ■ 73 Khan Market
■ 98108 77701 ■ Open noon–
11:30pm daily ■ ₹₹

A quirky, old-fashioned Bombay Parsi
restaurant *(see p65)*, successfully
re-created in Delhi.

*See map on pp92–3*

# TOP 10 South Delhi

The upwardly mobile suburbs of South Delhi are where visitors will find what makes modern Delhi tick, with a string of upmarket neighbourhoods, suave restaurants and glitzy modern malls. Despite its contemporary appearance, South Delhi was once home to the city's earliest settlements, and many of its oldest monuments can be found here. Most of these date back to the Delhi sultans, whose various forts, mosques and wonderful mausoleums still stand scattered majestically amongst modern suburbia. The highlight is the Qutb Minar complex and the adjacent Mehrauli Archaeological Park, while there are further memorable attractions at both Tughlaqabad and Hauz Khas.

**Baha'i Temple**

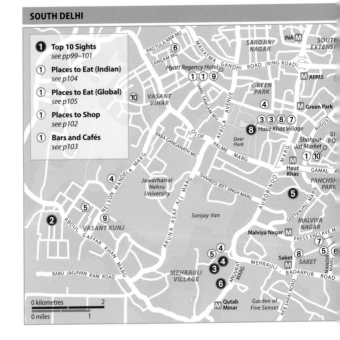

**SOUTH DELHI**

1️⃣ **Top 10 Sights**
see pp99–101

① **Places to Eat (Indian)**
see p104

① **Places to Eat (Global)**
see p105

① **Places to Shop**
see p102

① **Bars and Cafés**
see p103

### 1 Baha'i Temple

MAP X2 ■ Kalkaji Mandir
Metro ■ Open summer: 9am–7pm
Tue–Sun; winter: 9am–5:30pm Tue–
Sun ■ www.bahaihouseofworship.in

Completed in 1986 to a design by
Iranian architect Fariborz Sahba,
the Baha'i Temple is Delhi's most
striking modern building. Popularly
known as the Lotus Temple, the
design was inspired by the image
of an unfolding lotus flower, with
27 huge white petals emerging from
nine pools, symbolizing the nine
spiritual paths of the Baha'i faith.

### 2 Tomb of Sultan Ghari

MAP T3 ■ Malakpur village,
Vasant Kunj ■ Taxi or auto-rickshaw
■ Open 7am–5pm daily

Marooned on the outskirts of the city,
this impressive but little-visited tomb
was built in 1231 by Iltutmish for his
son and heir Nasiruddin Mahmud
following the latter's premature
death. It is the oldest Islamic tomb in
India, looking more like a fort than a
mausoleum. The name Sultan Ghari
means "Royal Cave", referring to the
troglodytic burial chamber beneath
the central octagonal platform. The
tomb is an architectural curiosity,
as much Hindu as Muslim in style.

### 3 Quwwat-ul-Islam

The centrepiece of the Qutb
Minar complex, the Quwwat-ul-Islam
(see p24) was the subcontinent's first
mosque, begun by Aibak and extended
by his successors, including Alauddin
Khilji (see p45), who added the fine
Alai Darwaza red sandstone gateway
in 1311. Inside, the prayer-hall
screen, covered in Koranic carvings,
is one of India's finest early examples of Islamic architecture.

### 4 Qutb Minar

One of Delhi's most iconic
sights, the soaring Qutb Minar (see
pp24–5) towers over the southern
city: a vast minaret begun during
the reign of the first Delhi sultan
Qutbuddin Aibak. The design is
quite unlike anything else in the
subcontinent, more Afghan than
Indian, with angular projecting
flanges punctuated by balconies
and bands of Koranic script.

**Column detail at Qutb Minar**

**Domes at Begumpuri Masjid**

## 5 Begumpuri and Khirki Masjids

MAP V2 ■ Malviya Nagar ■ Malviya Nagar Metro ■ Open sunrise–sunset daily

The Begumpuri, with its arcaded courtyard topped by domes, and the Khirki, with its tapering shape and almost completely covered courtyard, are typical of the 14th-century Tughlaq era.

## 6 Mehrauli Village and Archaeological Park

MAP U3 ■ Mehrauli ■ Qutab Minar Metro ■ Open sunrise–sunset daily

The Mehrauli Archaeological Park *(see p27)* and adjacent village of Mehrauli are home to an extraordinary collection of ancient monuments, dating from the 13th to the 19th centuries. There is a rich cluster of Mughal monuments, ranging from the Jamali-Kamali Masjid to the Zafar Mahal, and notable Sultanate-era attractions such as the Jahaz Mahal and the serene *dargah* of the Sufi saint Qutb Sahib, buried away in the depths of the village.

## 7 Ashoka's Rock Edict

MAP X2 ■ Off Raja Dhirsain Marg, Kailash Hills ■ Open 24 hrs

Not far from the Baha'i Temple lies a large boulder *(see p51)*, carved with a faint tracery of fading Brahmi script. This is one of the city's three monuments dating from the time of the Mauryan Emperor Ashoka. Ashoka converted to Buddhism early in his reign, and erected, across the country, a series of pillars and rock edicts on which his various proclamations were recorded. Unlike the city's two Ashokan columns, this rock edict stands on its original site.

## 8 Hauz Khas Village

MAP U2 ■ Hauz Khas Village ■ Taxi, auto-rickshaw or Green Park Metro ■ Open 24 hrs

The upmarket village of Hauz Khas is home to a string of ancient monuments, the Deer Park *(see p58)* and a number of eating and shopping venues. The village is centred around a reservoir, the Hauz-i-Alai, built by Alauddin Khilji in 1304. The sequence of buildings girding the lake was added half a century later.

**Monuments at Mehrauli Village**

### URBAN VILLAGES

Scattered amid South Delhi's suburbs are the remains of many formerly isolated villages that have now been swallowed up by the advancing urban tide. The most notable ones are Hauz Khas, Nizamuddin, Chiragh and Mehrauli. Each is home to an important *dargah* and retains its original street layout.

**⑨ Chiragh Delhi**
MAP W2 ▪ Lal Bahadur Shastri Marg ▪ Chirag Delhi Metro

Now engulfed by suburban sprawl, the ancient village of Chiragh Delhi has managed to preserve much of its traditional atmosphere, retaining parts of the walls that once surrounded it. The main attraction here is the *dargah* of Roshan Chiragh Delhi, while the tomb of Delhi sultan, Buhlul Lodi, lies outside the village.

**Citadel ruins at Tughlaqabad**

**⑩ Tughlaqabad**
MAP X3 ▪ Mehrauli-Badarpur Road ▪ Taxi, auto-rickshaw or Govindpuri Metro ▪ Open sunrise–sunset daily ▪ Adm and charge for video

Constructed during the reign of Ghiyasuddin Tughlaq, Tughlaqabad *(see p50)* was the third city of Delhi, dwarfing the previous settlements of Siri and Lal Kot, with a string of fortified ramparts and city walls stretching for 6 km (4 miles). The walls and citadel within are now in ruins, but still impressive and worth a visit. Just over the road lies the austere tomb of Ghiyasuddin himself.

## A DAY IN SOUTH DELHI

### ▶ MORNING

South Delhi's attractions are spread out, and you will need to take transport between the various sites. You could pick up auto-rickshaws between each stop, though it is easiest to hire a knowledgeable taxi- or auto-rickshaw-driver for the day to ferry you around.

Start the day with an hour or so at the remarkable **Qutb Minar Complex** *(see p99)* and spend the rest of the morning exploring the monuments of the **Mehrauli Archaeological Park** and the adjacent **Mehrauli Village**. Next, head to the excellent **Garden of Five Senses** *(see p58)* and have lunch at **Olive Bar & Kitchen** *(see p105)*.

### AFTERNOON

After lunch, head north, taking in some of Delhi's least-visited but most absorbing monuments, including the **Begumpuri Masjid**. Stop in the fascinating urban village of **Chiragh Delhi** to visit the *dargah*. If you have time, go to the **Khirki Masjid** and nearby **Lal Gumbad** *(see p44)*. Then, drive over towards Hauz Khas. Visit the beautiful reservoir and surrounding buildings, the **Deer Park**, and then explore the quiet streets of **Hauz Khas Village** and its superb boutique shops. Continue north to the **Baha'i Temple** *(see p99)*, aiming to arrive in the evening when the lighting makes it look spectacular. Finally, make your way to **Masjid Moth** in Greater Kailash II for a meal at **Oh! Calcutta** *(see p104)*.

*See map on pp98–9* ←

# Places to Shop

**(1) Shahpur Jat Market**
MAP V2 ▪ Shahpur Jat, Siri Fort
▪ Open daily (timings vary)
Vintage and contemporary clothing, accessories, jewellery, rugs and home decor are all on offer in the trendy new fashion boutiques of this chic urban village.

**(2) Kilol**
MAP W2 ▪ 4-N Block Market, Greater Kailash I ▪ 2924 3388
▪ Open 10:30am–8pm daily
A lovely store specializing in reasonably priced, hand block-printed fabrics from Jaipur.

**(3) Tatsat**
MAP U2 ▪ E-50 Main Market, Hauz Khas ▪ 4165 5792 ▪ Open 10am–8pm Mon–Sat, noon–8pm Sun
Tatsat sells garments, accessories, recycled goods, stationery and colourful hand-painted *chai* glasses and kettles, all sourced from eco-friendly organizations.

**(4) DLF Emporio**
MAP T2 ▪ 4 Nelson Mandela Marg, Vasant Kunj ▪ 4611 6666
▪ Open 11am–9pm daily
Delhi's most deluxe shopping mall, where affluent Delhiites come to buy designerwear from all the top international brands.

**(5) Ravissant**
MAP X1 ▪ 50–51 Grandlay Commercial Complex, New Friends Colony ▪ 2683 7278 ▪ Open 10am–7pm Mon–Sat ▪ www.ravissant.in
A sophisticated store with beautiful "Indian-inspired" clothes in breezy fabrics, home decor and silverware.

**(6) Abraham & Thakore**
MAP W1 ▪ Ist floor, D-25 Defence Colony ▪ 4155 2540
▪ Open 11am–7pm Mon–Sat
▪ www.abrahamandthakore.com
A Delhi fashion institution best known for its classic cuts and pristine natural fabrics.

**(7) Nalli**
MAP V1 ▪ G-16 South Extension II ▪ 95389 22277 ▪ Open 10am–8:30pm daily
Established in 1928, Nalli is popular for its traditional silk saris.

**(8) Utsav**
MAP W2 ▪ 3 Krishi Vihar Complex ▪ 2624 2420 ▪ Open 11am–7:30pm Mon–Sat
Utsav stocks saris in every possible fabric imaginable, plus accessories.

**Exquisite Fabindia furnishings**

**(9) Fabindia**
MAP W2 ▪ 7-N Block Market, Greater Kailash I ▪ 4669 3706 ▪ Open 10am–8pm daily
Fabindia stocks everything from furniture and natural cosmetics to organic food and clothes.

**(10) Apartment 9**
MAP W2 ▪ 9, N Block Market, Greater Kailash I ▪ 4902 9286 ▪ Open 10am–7:30pm daily
Shop for perfect home decor and accessories that combine contemporary design with a touch of old-world charm.

# Bars and Cafés

**1** **Polo Lounge**
MAP U1 ▪ Hyatt Regency, Bhikaji Cama Place ▪ 2679 1234 ▪ Open 11am–1am daily
Step back in time at this plush, England-inspired bar.

**2** **Cirrus 9**
MAP R5 ▪ The Oberoi, Dr Zakir Hussain Marg ▪ 2430 4370 ▪ Open 5pm–1am
The rooftop bar *(see p65)* at the Oberoi Hotel offers views of the Delhi Golf Course and Humayun's Tomb.

**3** **Social**
MAP U2 ▪ 9-A & 12, Hauz Khas Village ▪ 78386 52814 ▪ Open 11am–midnight daily
A popular restaurant-bar, Social *(see p65)* serves a range of global dishes, creative cocktails and some of the best breakfasts in Delhi.

**4** **The Piano Man**
MAP V2 ▪ B-6-7/22 Safdarjung Enclave Market ▪ 4131 5181 ▪ Open noon–12:45am daily
This club, with a grand piano and an intimate bar, is a great place for live jazz performances and cocktails.

**5** **Monkey Bar**
MAP T2 ▪ Plot 11 Upper Ground Floor, LSC, Pocket C-6 & 7, Vasant Kunj ▪ 4109 5155 ▪ Open 1pm–midnight daily
A hip new bar with a touch of the gastropub and great cocktails.

**6** **The Chatter House**
MAP W2 ▪ S 2-3 & F-15, Lower Ground Floor, Epicuria Mall, inside Nehru Place Metro Station ▪ 85888 44116 ▪ Open noon–1am daily
With a lively ambience in a brick and wood interior, this place has a full bar and serves classic cocktails.

**7** **Shalom – Laidback Café**
MAP W2 ▪ 10-N Block Market, Greater Kailash I ▪ 98100 48084 ▪ Open noon–1am daily
Live music, paired with great cocktails, make this spot one of the city's most popular nightclubs.

**8** **Imperfecto**
MAP V2 ▪ A1/1 Hauz Khas Village ▪ 96430 02717 ▪ Open noon–midnight daily
This charming café with good vibes has a variety of innovative Indian and European delicacies on the menu.

**9** **Artisan Lab**
MAP W2 ▪ N 18, N Block, Greater Kailash I ▪ 96676 22267 ▪ Open 11am–8:30pm daily
The seasonal menu at Artisan Lab features fresh, sustainable food.

**10** **PCO**
MAP T3 ▪ 4-D Block Market, Vasant Vihar ▪ 97111 08482 ▪ Open 5:30pm–12:30am daily
This "speakeasy", with a secret entry code and retro decor, serves inventive cocktails.

**The cosy interior of PCO, a popular South Delhi bar**

*See map on pp98–9*

# Places to Eat (Indian)

 **Swagath**
MAP W1 ▪ 14 Main Market, Defence Colony ▪ 2433 0930 ▪ Open 11am–midnight daily ▪ ₹₹

Swagath is known for serving some of the most delicious south Indian fare in town.

The colourful entrance to Naivedyam

**Oh! Calcutta**
MAP W2 ▪ Local Shopping Centre Masjid Moth, Greater Kailash II ▪ 93101 49806 ▪ Open 12:30–3:30pm & 7:30–10:30pm daily ▪ ₹₹

Exuding old-world charm, this restaurant specializes in excellent traditional Bengali fare.

**Carnatic Café**
MAP X1 ▪ Community Centre, New Friends Colony ▪ 4100 8630 ▪ Open 9am–10:30pm daily ▪ ₹

Innovative dosas and fabulous filter coffee is served here at reasonable prices.

 **Sagar Ratna**
MAP W1 ▪ 18 Defence Colony Market ▪ 2433 3658 ▪ Open 8am–11pm daily ▪ ₹

This canteen-style restaurant serves vegetarian south Indian cuisine.

**Dakshin**
MAP V3 ▪ Sheraton New Delhi, Saket ▪ 4266 1122 ▪ Open 12:30–2:45pm & 7:30–11:45pm daily ▪ ₹₹₹

Elegant and unassuming, Dakshin serves the best Malayali food in the city.

 **Delhi Club House**
MAP U1 ▪ Sangam Courtyard, R K Puram ▪ 97175 35533 ▪ Open noon–12:30am daily ▪ ₹₹

This restaurant-bar offers a curated selection of signature dishes from clubhouses across India.

**Naivedyam**
MAP U2 ▪ Hauz Khas Village ▪ Open 10am–10:30pm ▪ 4175 4984 ▪ ₹

Known for its cosy ambience and quick service, this place offers south Indian cuisine on a budget.

**Juggernaut**
MAP W2 ▪ HS-16, Kailash Colony Market ▪ 4131 9991 ▪ Open 6am–11pm daily ▪ ₹

With its fun, unconventional decor and innovative menu, this spot has become popular with the local crowd for south Indian meals.

**Fabcafé**
MAP T3 ▪ Shop 10, Sector B, Vasant Kunj ▪ 3310 6192 ▪ Open 10am–11pm daily ▪ ₹₹

A product of Fabindia (see p102), this modern Indian bistro is all about locally-grown organic produce, and even offers a vegan menu.

Malayali cuisine at Dakshin

**Potbelly Rooftop Cafe**
MAP V2 ▪ 116-C, 4th Floor, Shahpur Jat ▪ 4161 2048 ▪ Open noon–11pm daily ▪ ₹₹

The mouth-watering Bihari cuisine served at this rooftop restaurant includes *litti chokha* – a roasted dough ball stuffed with *sattu* (roasted chickpea flour) – served with mashed roast aubergine and potato.

# Places to Eat (Global)

### 1 The China Kitchen
MAP U1 ▪ Hyatt Regency, Bhikaji Cama Place ▪ 6677 1334 ▪ Open noon–3pm & 7–11:30pm daily ▪ ₹₹₹

A culinary milestone for Chinese food in the city, the food here (see p65) is complemented with stylish interiors.

### 2 Yum Yum Cha
MAP V3 ▪ A3 Select Citywalk, Saket ▪ 4155 3030 ▪ Open noon–11pm daily ▪ ₹₹

A laid-back Japanese restaurant, Yum Yum Cha serves amazing dim sum, sushi and wok creations in an origami inspired setting.

### 3 Diva
MAP W2 ▪ 8A, M Block Market, Greater Kailash II ▪ 2921 5673 ▪ Open 12:30–11:30pm daily ▪ ₹₹₹

This quiet, understated restaurant serves arguably the best Italian food in town. Sunday brunch is popular.

### 4 Qla
MAP U3 ▪ 4-A, Seven Style Mile, Kalka Das Marg, Mehrauli ▪ 85279 33766 ▪ Open noon–midnight daily ▪ ₹₹₹

A fine-dining restaurant, Qla serves European-influenced cuisine in an old *haveli* (mansion). The courtyard is ideal for sunny brunches and atmospheric dinners.

### 5 Olive Bar & Kitchen
MAP U3 ▪ 6, One Style Mile, Kalka Das Marg, Mehrauli ▪ 98102 35472 ▪ Open 12:30am–12:30pm daily ▪ ₹₹₹

Set in a *haveli*, Olive (see p64) offers light Italian and Mediterranean fare.

### 6 Burma Burma
MAP V3 ▪ S-25, Select Citywalk, Saket ▪ 4914 5807 ▪ Open noon–4pm & 6:30–10:30pm Mon–Fri, noon–10:30pm Sat & Sun ▪ ₹₹

Enjoy contemporary Burmese cuisine along with a selection of teas here.

### 7 Smoke House Deli
MAP U2 ▪ 252/253, DLF Place Mall, Saket ▪ 4061 2823 ▪ Open 11am–midnight daily ▪ ₹₹

This European restaurant focuses on smoked and grilled meats.

### 8 Lebanese Point
MAP V3 ▪ Shop 7 Ground Floor, PVR Anupam Shopping Complex, Saket ▪ 4166 4440 ▪ Open noon–11:30pm daily ▪ ₹

Head to Lebanese Point for the best chicken shawarmas in town; decent falafel and mezze, too.

### 9 La Piazza
MAP U1 ▪ Hyatt Regency ▪ 6677 1310 ▪ Open noon–3pm & 7–11:30pm daily ▪ ₹₹₹

Fresh, hearty Italian dishes are served here amid relaxed surroundings.

### 10 Fio Cookhouse & Bar
MAP W2 ▪ Epicuria Mall, Nehru Place Metro Station ▪ 99710 04536 ▪ Open 12:30pm–12:30am daily ▪ ₹₹₹

European and Indian cuisine, plus inventive cocktails are on offer here.

**The stylish interiors at Fio**

# Streetsmart

**Auto-rickshaws parked in New Delhi**

| Getting Around | 108 |
| Practical Information | 110 |
| Places to Stay | 114 |
| General Index | 120 |
| Acknowledgments | 126 |
| Selected Street Index | 128 |

# Getting Around

## Arriving by Air

The city's **Indira Gandhi International Airport** has three main terminals – T3 handles international and some domestic flights (carriers include **Air India**, **Air Canada**, **Jet Airways**, **British Airways**, **Virgin Atlantic** and **United Airlines**). T1 and T2 are for arrival and departure of low-cost domestic flights (airlines include **IndiGo** and **SpiceJet**). There are direct flights to Delhi from all major hubs, including London, Toronto, New York and Sydney. All three terminals are connected via a 24x7 free bus service that runs every 20 minutes; you need to show your flight ticket before boarding. The fastest way into the city from T3 is via the Airport Express Line (5am–11pm) of the Delhi Metro, which takes 20 minutes to reach New Delhi railway station (Ajmeri Gate side). From T1 there's a connecting shuttle (6am–10pm) to Delhi Aerocity station.

A 24-hour bus service connects both terminals to Connaught Place, New Delhi Station (Ajmeri Gate side), the Red Fort and Maharana Pratap ISBT (40 minutes). For taxis, there are pre-paid taxi kiosks in the arrivals area, but prices vary, so check a few.

## Arriving by Train

The most convenient train station for visitors is New Delhi, which, despite its name, is located between New Delhi and Old Delhi. Some services from northern India use Delhi Junction at the northern end of Old Delhi. Many from the south (including some from Agra) use Hazrat Nizamuddin, south of the centre, while those from the east may terminate at Anand Vihar, and those from Rajasthan terminate at Sarai Rohilla.

New Delhi and Anand Vihar have metro stations. Delhi Junction is served by Chandni Chowk metro. There is another metro station at Hazrat Nizamuddin. All rail terminals have kiosks for pre-paid auto-rickshaw fares.

For the city of Agra, the most convenient service is the 6am Bhopal Shatabdi Express from New Delhi, returning from Agra Cantonment station at 9:15pm.

Foreign tourists should buy their tickets from the **Foreigners' Booking Office** on the upper floor of New Delhi station (bring your passport). Staff can advise on the best trains to use, or you can check the **Indian Railways** website for timetables or call the **Railway Enquiries** phone number. Ignore anyone who tells you that the office has closed or volunteers directions to it (almost certainly with the intention of directing you to a crooked travel agent).

## Long-Distance Bus Travel

Travelling by bus or coach means you often have a wider choice of timings, stops and itineraries; plus, buses can get to places that trains do not reach.

There are three main intercity bus stations – Maharana Pratap ISBT (Intercity State Bus Terminal) in Old Delhi, Anand Vihar ISBT and Rajasthan Roadways. Tickets don't need to be pre-booked for regular bus services, but bookings may be required for certain routes on deluxe buses; travellers can reserve tickets through travel agencies such as **redBus** and **MakeMyTrip**.

## Metro and Bus

The **Delhi Metro**, which runs from 5am until midnight, is the most convenient way of getting around the city. Trains run every two to four minutes, and tickets are cheap. Rechargeable Smart Cards save time and are worth getting if you intend to use the metro during your trip. Women have reserved seats, as well as the first carriage to themselves, which is a good option to use during peak hours. Baggage is limited to 15 kg (33 lb), or 60 cm x 45 cm x 25 cm (23.5 in x 17.5 in x 10 in).

**DTC** (Delhi Transport Corporation) has a good bus network. Routes can be confusing, and vehicles may be very crowded, but at times the service can be very handy. Their website can tell you the best route between any two stops, but you will need to know their correct names.

"One", a common mobility card, can be used for both Metro and DTC buses, and can be found at all metro stations.

## Taxis

Your hotel should be able to book you a cab, but otherwise it's best to hire one from a local stand. Metered radio cabs are a good option, but they cost a little more – **Meru Cabs, Mega Cabs** and **Quick Cabs** can be booked online, by phone, or via their apps. You can book taxis online through apps such as **Ola** and **Uber. BluSmart** is India's first all-electric cab service. The booking app enables users to schedule cabs up to 48 hours in advance.

## Auto-Rickshaws

Auto-rickshaws ("autos") are the standard way of getting around Delhi. They are fitted with meters, but most drivers don't use them and you may have to bargain. Know what price you want to pay before stopping an auto, and agree on a fare before boarding. Fares should be ₹25 for the first two kilometres then roughly ₹8 per kilometre. You can avoid bargaining to ensure you don't get overcharged by hiring pre-paid autos at set rates from kiosks in Connaught Place, at Janpath (outside the tourism office) and at major transport terminals. Both Ola and Uber offer an option to pre-book autos as well.

## Cycle Rickshaws

Cycle rickshaws are a great way to get around the old city. Fares are about half those of an auto, but again, haggling is the order of the day. These are banned from Connaught Place and central New Delhi. *Rickshawwallahs* are some of Delhi's poorest: if they do a good job, be generous.

## Walking

While some pockets of the city are good for exploring on foot, it is best if you are aware of your surroundings at all times. Honking on roads is very common so don't be alarmed. Look to either side of the road before crossing as people often drive on the wrong side. Major roads have foot over bridges and underpasses (subways), so make sure to use them when possible.

## DIRECTORY

### ARRIVING BY AIR

**Air Canada**
📞 4717 2900
🌐 aircanada.com

**Air India**
📞 1 860 233 1407
🌐 airindia.in

**British Airways**
📞 0124 412 0715
🌐 britishairways.com

**IndiGo**
📞 0124 617 3838
🌐 goindigo.in

**Indira Gandhi International Airport**
📞 0124 337 6000
🌐 newdelhiairport.in

**Jet Airways**
📞 3989 3333
🌐 jetairways.com

**SpiceJet**
📞 0124 498 3410
🌐 spicejet.com

**United Airlines**
📞 0124 431 5500
🌐 united.com

**Virgin Atlantic**
📞 0124 469 3030
🌐 virgin-atlantic.com

### ARRIVING BY TRAIN

**Foreigners' Booking Office**
New Delhi Railway Station, Upper Floor; 8am–8pm Mon–Sat, 8am–2pm Sun
📞 2334 6804

**Indian Railways**
🌐 indianrail.gov.in

**Railway Enquiries**
📞 1 800 111 139
🌐 enquiry.indianrail. gov.in/ntes

### LONG-DISTANCE BUS TRAVEL

**MakeMyTrip**
🌐 makemytrip.com

**redBus**
🌐 redbus.in

### METRO AND BUS

**Delhi Metro**
📞 2341 7910
🌐 delhimetrorail.com

**DTC**
📞 1 800 118 181
🌐 dtcbusroutes.in

### TAXIS

**BluSmart**
📞 1 8007 005 005
🌐 blu-smart.com

**Mega Cabs**
📞 90909 09090
🌐 megacabs.com

**Meru Cabs**
📞 4422 4422
🌐 merucabs.com

**Ola**
🌐 olacabs.com

**Quick Cabs**
📞 6767 6767
🌐 quickcabservices.co.in

**Uber**
🌐 uber.com/cities/ new-delhi

# Practical Information

## Passports and Visas

For entry requirements, including visas, consult your nearest Indian embassy or check the **India Visa Online** website. Almost all nationalities require a visa. Tourist visas are valid from 30 days to 5 years, depending on the type and e-Visa is available for nationals of certain countries. For a longer stay, you'll need to apply in person or by post at the nearest Visa Office or alternatively at the Indian High Commission – there is a list of the latter on the website of the **Ministry of External Affairs**.

## Government Advice

Consult both your and the Indian government's advice before travelling. The **UK Foreign, Commonwealth & Development Office (FCDO)**, the **US State Department** and the **Australian Department of Foreign Affairs and Trade** offer the latest information on security, health and local regulations.

## Customs Information

For laws relating to goods and currency taken in or out of India check the **Central Board of Indirect Taxes & Customs (CBIC)** website.

## Insurance

We recommend that you take out a comprehensive insurance policy covering theft, loss of belongings, medical care, cancellations and delays, and read the small print carefully.

## Health

Delhi's heathcare system is good but quality in medical treatments will vary in rural and urban areas as well as in public and private hospitals. The **US Embassy Delhi Doctors List** is useful. Vaccinations against meningitis, typhoid, tetanus and hepatitis A are recommended. Make sure that you are covered against polio. Malaria and dengue fever outbreaks can occur, especially in and after the monsoon months (Jul–Sep); use high-DEET or PMD mosquito repellent.

Avoid food that is not freshly cooked, even unpeeled fruit unless you can clean it. In case of stomach upsets, drink plenty of fluids and stick to plain boiled food until the sickness subsides, or consult a doctor. **AIIMS** (All India Institute of Medical Sciences) is one of the country's top research hospitals; other hospitals include **Dr Ram Manohar Lohia Hospital**, the **East West Medical Centre** and chains such as **Apollo Hospitals** and **Max Healthcare**. The **Apollo Pharmacy** in Connaught Place is open 24 hours. For information regarding COVID-19 vaccination requirements, consult government advice.

## Smoking, Alcohol and Drugs

Delhi has numerous dry days. Smoking is banned in public places, and in places of worship. India produces hashish and marijuana bud, but both are illegal with harsh penalties in force for possession. *Bhang* (marijuana leaf) is legally sold in licensed shops in some cities.

## ID

There is no requirement to carry or show ID in India, and passports can usually be left in a hotel safe. It is nonetheless a good idea to keep a photo of your passport on your phone. You will need your passport to make train reservations.

## Personal Security

Travelling in Delhi is relatively safe, but it is recommended that you follow a few simple precautions. Wear a money belt under your shirt and be discreet with your camera and phone. While shopping, ensure shopkeepers make out a bill and process card transactions in front of you. Never accept food or drink from strangers, especially on public transport. Keep your baggage close at transport terminals and beware of staged distractions; padlock your luggage to the chain beneath your seat during train journeys.

Although "eve-teasing" (sexual harassment) is a punishable offence, women – both Indian and foreign – face unwanted male attention on a daily basis, and there have been incidents of rape and violence against female travellers. Avoid walking alone in isolated places and in the rougher parts of cities, or taking buses at night. When hiring a car or taxi, ask your hotel to book it for you (or go to a cab rank) and note the licence plate number. When queuing for train or cinema tickets, use the "ladies' lines", and use the "ladies only" seats or compartments on buses and trains, if available. If you feel unsafe, reach out to your nearest consulate, or contact the police by calling the **Tourist Helpline** or the **Womens' Helpline**.

Over the past few years laws banning homosexuality have been overturned as unconstitutional, but marriage equality is still under litigation. LGBTQ+ travellers should note that India is a conservative country, so it is best to avoid public displays of affection. If you feel unsafe, call the **Nazariya Foundation** helpline for the nearest place of refuge.

## Travellers with Specific Requirements

The city can be challenging for the differently abled, but things are improving. Old Delhi is hard-going in a wheelchair, but New Delhi has more facilities. The metro stations are accessible and have tactile paths for people with visual impairment. Major sights and museums make some effort, with ramps and accessible toilets. HoHo tour buses (see p109) are accessible and some with lifts have been added to the DTC fleet. Hotels are unlikely to have wheelchair-adapted rooms, and those that do will tend to be at the top of the market – some are listed on **Disabled Access Holidays**. In the UK, **Disabled Holidays** offers package tours to the region for people with limited mobility.

## DIRECTORY

### PASSPORTS AND VISAS

**India Visa Online**
w indianvisaonline.gov.in

**Ministry of External Affairs**
w mea.gov.in

### GOVERNMENT ADVICE

**Australian Department of Foreign Affairs and Trade**
w smartraveller.gov.au

**UK Foreign, Commonwealth & Development Office (FCDO)**
w gov.uk/foreign-travel-advice

**US State Department**
w travel.state.gov

### CUSTOMS INFORMATION

**Central Board of Indirect Taxes & Customs (CBIC)**
w cbic.gov.in/entities/internationalTravellers

### HEALTH

**AIIMS**
Aurobindo Marg
C 6590 0669
w aiims.edu

**Apollo Hospitals**
w apollohospitals.com

**Apollo Pharmacy**
G-8 Connaught Place
C 2371 1838

**Dr Ram Manohar Lohia Hospital**
Baba Kharak Singh Marg
C 2340 4286
w rmlh.nic.in

**East West Medical Centre**
38 Golf Links
C 2469 9229
w eastwestrescue.com

**Max Healthcare**
C 4055 4055
w maxhealthcare.in

### US Embassy Delhi Doctors List
w in.usembassy.gov/u-s-citizen-services/local-resources-of-u-s-citizens/doctors

### PERSONAL SECURITY

**Nazariya Foundation**
w thenazariyafoundation.org

**Tourist Helpline**
C 87508 71111

**Womens' Helpline**
C 1091

### TRAVELLERS WITH SPECIFIC REQUIREMENTS

**Disabled Access Holidays**
w disabledaccessholidays.com

**Disabled Holidays**
w disabledholidays.com

## Time Zone

Delhi is on India Standard Time (IST), which is 5.5 hours ahead of London, 9.5 hours ahead of New York, 12.5 hours ahead of Los Angeles, and 4.5 hours behind Sydney.

## Money

The local currency is rupees (₹), which come in notes of ₹2,000, ₹500, ₹200, ₹100, ₹50, ₹20, ₹10 and occasionally still ₹5, with coins of ₹20, ₹10, ₹5, ₹2 and ₹1. It is illegal to import or export Indian currency. If you have over US$10,000 in foreign currency, you must declare it.

Banks are open from 10am to mid-afternoon Monday to Friday, plus a couple of hours on first, third and fifth Saturday mornings. Private bureaux de change are becoming quite common, especially in Connaught Place and Paharhanj, and may offer decent rates. Mid- and upper-range hotels exchange foreign currency, but often at poor rates. ATMs are common and accept foreign-issued credit and debit cards (especially MasterCard and Visa). These are widely accepted in upmarket shops and restaurants, but may have an extra charge.

## Electrical Appliances

The electricity supply is 230V 50Hz AC. Most sockets are triple round-pin but take European-size double round-pin plugs. British,

Irish and Australasian devices will only need an adaptor. North American devices will need an adaptor and a converter.

## Mobile Phones and Wi-Fi

The country code for India is +91; the area code for Delhi is 011. If you are planning to use your mobile in Delhi, check rates and accessibility with your service provider in your home country. SIM cards for mobile phones are widely available, but you will need your passport to buy one.

Most hotels provide Wi-Fi access, and many bars, restaurants, cafés and malls provide free Wi-Fi, there are also a few free Wi-Fi zones in the city. For internet cafés try **Sunrise** and **Cyber Floor** at Connaught Place.

## Postal Services

There is a branch of the **Post Office** at Connaught Place. For poste restante, you will need to go to the **General Post Office** (GPO), near Connaught Place. Sending letters and postcards is easy, but packages do need to be sealed.

## Weather

It is best to visit Delhi in spring (February–April) or autumn (mid-September–November). It is extremely hot in May and June (temperatures reach 45°C/113°F), rather wet from late June until mid-September, when monsoon kicks in, and

gets quite chilly in December and January, when temperatures can dip below 5°C (41°F).

## Opening Hours

Shops typically open 10am–6pm Monday to Saturday. Many museums and some tourist sights are closed on Mondays.

The COVID-19 pandemic proved that situations can change suddenly. Always check before visiting attractions and hospitality venues for up-to-date hours and booking requirements.

## Visitor Information

**India Tourism** and **Delhi Tourism** (DTTDC) have offices off Connaught Place, and Delhi Tourism has offices at the airport and bus and train stations. **Delhi Diary**, free at the India Tourism office, lists exhibitions and cultural events, while **Time Out Delhi** has entertainment listings. Online, check out **Delhi Capital** and **Little Black Book**.

## Local Customs

Eat with your right hand only, as the left hand is reserved for practical usages, like going to the toilet. It is customary to take off shoes (with the left hand) before entering a house. Putting feet up on furniture is considered bad manners, as is touching someone with your feet. If sitting on the floor, keep feet tucked underneath. Living in close quarters with family and neighbours gives Indians a different sense of "personal space" than many Westerners. If crowded or jostled, be tolerant as space is often at a premium.

Indians tend to dress conservatively and keep the body well covered. Wearing shorts is not common, and women wearing clothes that display their legs, arms or stomachs will draw stares and unwanted male attention.

## Language

The main language in this region is Hindi, which is India's official language, along with English. Other languages common in the region are Urdu and Punjabi, the latter spoken by many people in Delhi. English is widely used in India and around one in three people know at least some of it. Indian English is as distinctive as British, American or Australian, and has its own style, expressions and turns of phrase.

## Visiting Places of Worship

It is best to dress modestly when visiting places of worship; wear trousers that are at least knee-length and avoid sleeveless tops (women need to be covered from wrist to ankle). Remove shoes before entering a temple and if sitting, keep feet facing away from the main shrine. It is mandatory for everyone to cover their head before entering a gurdwara; head scarves are often available at the entrance. Jain temples do not allow leather items inside, even wallets and watch straps. A few Hindu temples also ban entry for non-Hindus. Women are not permitted in some Jain and Hindu temples, although this is controversial and some of these restrictions are being challenged in court.

Photography is prohibited in some temples and mosques so it's best to check on site before taking any pictures. Make sure to be respectful and accept any *prasad* (offerings) with your right hand.

## Taxes and Refunds

GST (Goods and Services Tax) is levied on all goods and services, typically at 18 per cent for non-essential items. It is included in displayed prices. While GST on souvenirs should be refundable to foreign residents on leaving the country, no mechanism for this has yet been put in place.

## Accommodation

Delhi has a huge range of accommodation, from five-star hotels to cheap backpacker lodges. Rates for mid-range accommodation are a bargain by Western standards. **MakeMyTrip** is very useful for locating unique places to stay. **Couchsurfing**, which allows travellers to book a short stay with a family, is also available in Delhi.

## DIRECTORY

**MOBILE PHONES AND WI-FI**

**Cyber Floor**
17 Scindia House, Connaught Place
📞 85859 78587

**Sunrise**
N-9/2, Connaught Place
📞 92129 35568

**POSTAL SERVICES**

**General Post Office**
Patel Chowk on Sansad Marg at Ashoka Road

**Post Office**
A-6 Connaught Place;
10am–7pm Mon–Sat

**VISITOR INFORMATION**

**Delhi Capital**
🔳 delhicapital.com

**Delhi Diary**
🔳 delhidiary.in

**Delhi Tourism**
Coffee Home, Baba Kharak Singh Marg
🔳 delhitourism.gov.in

**India Tourism**
88 Janpath
🔳 incredibleindia.org

**Little Black Book**
🔳 lbb.in/delhi

**Time Out Delhi**
🔳 timeout.com/delhi

**ACCOMMODATION**

**Couchsurfing**
🔳 couchsurfing.com

**MakeMyTrip**
🔳 makemytrip.com

# Places to Stay

**PRICE CATEGORIES**
For a standard, double room per night (with breakfast if included), taxes and extra charges.

₹ under ₹5,000    ₹₹ ₹5,000–15,000    ₹₹₹ over ₹15,000

## Luxury Hotels

### The Claridges
MAP N5 ■ 12 Dr APJ Abdul Kalam Road ■ 3955 5000 ■ www.claridges.com/hotels/the-claridges-new-delhi ■ ₹₹
A landmark in Lutyens's Delhi, Claridges is the epitome of old-world style. The building, with colonial-style pillars and high ceilings, has 137 rooms and suites as well as great restaurants. The Beatles stayed here in 1968.

### Hyatt Regency
MAP U1 ■ Bhikaji Cama Place ■ 2679 1234 ■ www.delhi.regency.hyatt.com ■ ₹₹
The Hyatt is ideal for those who like to feel the pulse of the city. The imposing structure has stylish and spacious rooms, a sleek club lounge and some excellent restaurants.

### The Lalit
MAP G6 ■ Barakhamba Avenue, Connaught Place ■ 4444 7777 ■ www.the lalit.com ■ ₹₹
Rooms are elegant and modern at this five-star hotel a few minutes away from Connaught Place. It is home to the chic nightclub Kitty Su (see p82).

### The Park
MAP F7 ■ 15 Parliament Street ■ 2374 3000 ■ www.theparkhotels.com ■ ₹₹
Contemporary art and design are the highlight of this hotel's decor, but the impeccable service and spacious rooms are welcome additions. Unwind at Aqua (see p82), which is set around a swimming pool.

### The Imperial
MAP F7 ■ 1 Janpath ■ 2334 1234 ■ www.the imperialindia.com ■ ₹₹₹
Opened in 1931, The Imperial is considered one of Asia's finest hotels. From its sweeping palm-lined drive to its classical white colonial structure, the place exudes quiet elegance and luxury. The walls are lined with a fine collection of European "traveller" paintings.

### ITC Maurya
MAP K4 ■ Diplomatic Enclave, Sardar Patel Marg ■ 2611 2233 ■ www.itchotels.in ■ ₹₹₹
Nestled in greenery, this is a delightful accommodation option due to its flawless service, location, forested Ridge views and excellent restaurant, Bukhara (see p65). It also houses beautiful artworks from eminent artists.

### The Lodhi
MAP Q6 ■ Lodi Road ■ 4363 3333 ■ www.thelodhi.com ■ ₹₹₹
The Lodhi combines modern decor with traditional touches such as Lodi-inspired jali screens and Khareda stone floors. The hotel has a great spa with Turkish hammam and private pools. The suites offer beautiful views.

### The Oberoi
MAP Q4 ■ Dr Zakir Hussain Marg ■ 2436 3030 ■ www.oberoi hotels.com ■ ₹₹₹
The Oberoi features rooms and suites inspired by the designs of Lutyens' New Delhi. It also offers views of the Delhi Golf Course and Humayun's Tomb (see p95).

### Oberoi Maidens
MAP G1 ■ 7 Sham Nath Marg ■ 2397 5464 ■ www.maidenshotel.com ■ ₹₹₹
Built in the early 1900s and nestled close to the city's leafy Civil Lines area, this beautiful white heritage building, with its colonial architectural style, retains a strong old-world charm.

### The Taj Mahal Hotel
MAP P4 ■ 1 Man Singh Road ■ 6656 6162 ■ www.taj.tajhotels.com ■ ₹₹₹
A lobby with Art Deco marble floors, fountains and beautiful mini-domes greets visitors to this hotel. The rooms are just as impressive, with decor that is a blend of traditional and contemporary.

### The Taj Palace
MAP K4 ■ 2 Sardar Patel Marg, Diplomatic Enclave ■ 2611 0202 ■ www.tajhotels.com ■ ₹₹₹
This grand building is set within lovely lawns and has striking interiors. Relax at the nine-hole chip-and-putt golf green or work out at the state-of-the-art fitness centre.

### Vivanta by Taj – Ambassador

MAP P5 ▪ Sujan Singh Park, Subramaniam Bharti Marg ▪ 6626 1000 ▪ www.seleqtionshotels.com/en-in/ambassador-new-delhi ▪ ₹₹₹

This centrally located hotel offers comfortable and stylish rooms, with classic interiors. The many highlights of staying here include a fitness centre that offers yoga, a popular on-site restaurant and a lovely breakfast buffet.

## Boutique Hotels

### Amarya Villa

MAP V1 ▪ A-2/20 Safdarjung Enclave ▪ 4103 6184 ▪ www.amaryagroup.com ▪ ₹₹

Conveniently located, this hotel is set away from the bustling crowds. It offers a range of spacious and stylish guestrooms that have been themed around the "Navratna", India's nine traditional auspicious gemstones.

### B Nineteen

MAP S6 ▪ B-19 Nizamuddin (East) ▪ 4182 5500 ▪ www.bnineteen.com ▪ ₹₹

A gorgeous boutique hotel, this blends tasteful contemporary style with traditional decor and wooden furniture. The service is non-intrusive, the food excellent and the location is top notch.

### Colonel's Retreat

MAP W1 ▪ D-418 Defence Colony ▪ 4660 4927 ▪ www.colonelsretreat.com ▪ ₹₹

Calling itself Delhi's "best-kept secret", this charming accommodation option feels a bit like staying in a friend's home. The terrace is the perfect place to relax and read a book or enjoy a meal.

### Haveli Dharampura

MAP G4 ▪ 2293 Gali Guliyan, Dharampura, near Jama Masjid Gate No. 3, Chandni Chowk ▪ 2326 1000 ▪ www.havelidharampura.com ▪ ₹₹

Set in an 1887 *haveli*, this wonderfully atmospheric hotel located in the bustling alleys of Old Delhi's Chandni Chowk is a short walk from the Jama Masjid and the Red Fort. The rooms are beautiful and the service is excellent.

### Udman Panchshila Park

MAP V2 ▪ N 82, Panchshila Park ▪ 4319 0000 ▪ www.udmanhotels.com ▪ ₹

With a contemporary yet understated design, this elegant hotel sits comfortably in its serene residential setting and provides a luxurious experience with a touch of Indian charm. The kitchen serves a delightful range of Indian and international dishes.

### Hotel Diplomat

MAP K4 ▪ 9 Sardar Patel Marg, Diplomatic Enclave ▪ 4605 0200 ▪ www.thehoteldiplomat.com ▪ ₹₹

Set amid sprawling green lawns, this hotel offers tastefully decorated rooms with contemporary interiors. The on-site restaurant, with a bistro vibe, is multi-cuisine and offers all-day breakfast and a view of the gardens.

### Jaypee Vasant Continental

MAP T2 ▪ Vasant Vihar ▪ 2614 8800 ▪ www.jaypeehotels.com/hotel/jaypee-vasant-continental-new-delhi ▪ ₹₹

Strategically located, this hotel blends business and leisure and offers modern accommodation. Amenities at the hotel include a swimming pool, health spa, fitness centre and a range of dining options.

### NUO by jüSTa Panchsheel Park

MAP V2 ▪ S-362 Panchsheel Park ▪ 4058 2121 ▪ www.justahotels.com/panchsheel-park-new-delhi ▪ ₹₹

This hotel offers spacious, well-furnished rooms with art-covered walls. The multicuisine restaurant serves tasty snacks and meals.

### La Sagrita

MAP R4 ▪ 14 Sundar Nagar ▪ 98100 67617 ▪ www.lasagrita.in ▪ ₹₹

This small but swanky boutique hotel is tucked away in a quiet neighbourhood between India Gate and Humayun's Tomb. The rooms are spacious and the breakfast is excellent.

### Lutyens Bungalow

MAP N6 ▪ 39 Prithviraj Road ▪ 2461 1341 ▪ www.lutyensbungalow.co.in ▪ ₹₹

Constructed in 1937, this charming bungalow is located in Central Delhi at a strolling distance from Lodi Gardens. There is a swimming pool to relax, and the living room is furnished with books and a fireplace for cool winter evenings.

### The Manor
MAP X1 ▪ 77 Friends Colony (West) ▪ 4130 7777 ▪ www.themanordelhi.com ▪ ₹₹
Established in 1999, this is Delhi's first boutique hotel. It is situated in a quiet corner of the upmarket Friends Colony, with the Ashram metro station within walking distance.

### The Muse Sarovar Portico
MAP W2 ▪ A-1 Chirag Enclave ▪ 4065 0000 ▪ www.sarovarhotels.com/the-muse-sarovar-portico-nehru-place-new-delhi ▪ ₹₹
The Muse is excellent for business travellers as it is conveniently located close to the IGI Airport and Nehru Place commercial complex. It has stylish rooms and excellent service.

### Mispah
MAP U1 ▪ B2-139 Safdarjung Enclave ▪ 93183 66090 ▪ www.mizpahdelhi.co.in ▪ ₹₹
This *maison d'hôte* offers four lovely rooms with French interiors blended with modern decor. It is the personal touch of the two French owners that makes this place stand out from other hotels.

### Thikana
MAP V2 ▪ A-7 Gulmohar Park ▪ 98101 43335 ▪ www.thikanadelhi.com ▪ ₹₹
Enjoy a stay at this hotel that offers rooms with traditional decor. The common areas have comfortable chairs, ideal for sinking into with a book or a drink. The property also has a lift for the ease of guests.

### Roseate House
MAP A6 ▪ Asset 10, Hospitality District, Aerocity ▪ 98188 08394 ▪ www.roseatehotels.com/newdelhi ▪ ₹₹
Located close to the airport, this hotel offers beautiful rooms and excellent service. Guests can relax at the outdoor and indoor spa, enjoy at the movie lounge or shop at the luxury brand stores.

## Mid-Range Hotels

### Bajaj Indian Homestay
MAP E5 ▪ 8A/34 Karol Bagh ▪ 2573 6509 ▪ www.indianhomestay.com ▪ ₹
The clean and spacious rooms at this homestay are named after Hindu gods as well as other mythological characters. There is also a charming terrace with views.

### BB Palace
MAP E5 ▪ 2638 Bank Street, Gurudwara Road, Karol Bagh ▪ 92055 73538 ▪ www.hotelbbpalace.com ▪ ₹
A friendly place with a few pleasant rooms. See the rooms before booking – those decorated with bright colours and dark wood furniture are lovely.

### Bloomrooms Hotel
MAP R7 ▪ 7 Link Road, Jangpura Extension ▪ 4122 5666 ▪ https://staybloom.com/hotels/delhi ▪ ₹
This is a great option located nearby popular sights such as the Lodi Gardens and Humayun's Tomb. The rooms are pleasant with minimalist and colourful decor. Amici Café here serves excellent all-day breakfast.

### Devna
MAP R4 ▪ 10 Sundar Nagar ▪ 98112 76231 ▪ www.devnadelhi.com ▪ ₹
Surrouned by greenery and located in a lovely neighbourhood, this guesthouse offers rooms decorated with antiques and paintings. There is a state-of-the-art gymnasium next door.

### Hamilton Hotel
MAP V2 ▪ S-153 Panchsheel Park ▪ 4168 6827 ▪ ₹
Located at the edge of Panchsheel Park, the Hamilton is ideally situated for exploring South Delhi's sights. The rooms are done up in bright colours, and there is a charming porch with a fountain where guests can unwind on comfortable cane chairs.

### Hotel Broadway
MAP H5 ▪ 4/15-A Asaf Ali Road ▪ 91215 80188 ▪ https://hotelbroadway.chobs.in ▪ ₹
Dating back to 1956 and sandwiched between Old Delhi and Connaught Place, Hotel Broadway has a certain endearing charm. The friendly staff can arrange activities for you, ranging from performances of traditional dance to walking tours through the old city.

### Hotel Florence
MAP E5 ▪ 2719 Bank Street, Karol Bagh ▪ 4502 5500 ▪ www.florencegroup.in ▪ ₹
A decent hotel offering comfortable rooms with clean en-suite bathrooms. An in-house restaurant serves Indian and some European dishes.

## Ahuja Residency

MAP Q5 ▪ 3 Sunder Nagar ▪ 4578 5000 ▪ www.ahuja residency.com ▪ ₹₹
Located in one of the city's most upmarket residential quarters, this is a good option for a quiet, relaxing stay. Efficient, non-intrusive service, beautiful room decor that blends the contemporary and traditional, a cosy dining space and all modern amenities, make Ahuja Residency a great place to stay.

## Hotel Palace Heights

MAP F6 ▪ D-26/28 Connaught Place ▪ 4546 0000 ▪ www.hotelpalace heights.com ▪ ₹₹
Tastefully decorated rooms with lovely paper blinds and warm, woody colours, an excellent restaurant and a great location are among the few reasons to stay at Palace Heights. The terrace restaurant is great for a beer and peppery chicken tikka.

## Ibis

MAP A6 ▪ Asset 9, Hospitality District, Delhi Aerocity ▪ 4302 0202 ▪ www.ibishotels. com ▪ ₹₹
Set near the airport, this chain hotel offers comfortable rooms with modern amenities. They also have a sumptuous breakfast buffet.

## Budget Hotels

### Blue Triangle Family Hostel (YWCA)

MAP E7 ▪ Ashoka Road ▪ 70112 99044 ▪ www. ywcaofdelhi.org ▪ ₹
This hostel provides safe and clean accommodation, particularly for women. There is a choice of double or single rooms, with en-suite baths and running hot water.

## Ginger Hotel

MAP G5 ▪ IRCTC – Rail Yatra, New Delhi Railway Station, Bhav Bhutti Marg ▪ 86026 63333 ▪ www.gingerhotels. com ▪ ₹
Winner of the CNBC travel award for the Best Budget Hotel, this place has spotlessly clean rooms, a gym, Wi-Fi and a restaurant.

## Hotel Mint Casa

MAP X1 ▪ Mint Casa, A-10, Friends Colony (East) ▪ 81919 00043 ▪ www.fabhotels.com ▪ ₹
The hotel has modern, comfortable rooms and efficient service. It is well located for exploring the sights of South Delhi.

## Hotel New Haven

MAP W2 ▪ E-512 Greater Kailash II ▪ 81309 92419 ▪ www.nhh.in ▪ ₹
This hotel has a good location in South Delhi and clean rooms. Guests can head to the nearby Greater Kailash market to choose from a variety of food options.

## Hotel Tara Palace

MAP H4 ▪ 419 Esplanade Road, Chandni Chowk ▪ 2327 6465 ▪ www. tarapalace.com ▪ ₹
With friendly service and a great location in the heart of Old Delhi, Hotel Tara Palace is the perfect starting point for exploring Chandni Chowk. Both the Red Fort and Jama Masjid are within walking distance of this hotel.

## International Youth Hostel

MAP K5 ▪ 5 Nyaya Marg, Chanakyapuri ▪ 2611 6285 ▪ www.yhaindia. org ▪ ₹
This is a huge favourite among young budget travellers for its location and facilities. Choose from a range of dorms, or double rooms with shared or private bathrooms.

## Madpackers

MAP V2 ▪ 3rd floor, S–39A Panchsheel Park ▪ 88002 65725 ▪ ₹
Conveniently located close to a metro station, this informal hostel has dorms, including one just for women, making it a good choice for female travellers. There are plenty of communal spaces, including a kitchen and a terrace.

## Metropolis Tourist Home

MAP F5 ▪ 1634, Main Bazar Road, Paharganj ▪ 2356 1782 ▪ www. metropolistouristhome. com ▪ ₹
Owing to its excellent location and friendly ser-vice, the Metropolis has fast become a popular budget option among backpackers. Located in the middle of busy Paharganj, it also has a great terrace restaurant.

## Stops

MAP H5 ▪ 4/23-B Asaf Ali Road ▪ 74288 82828 ▪ www.stopshostels. com ▪ ₹
Join the backpacker crowd at this cool hostel on the southern edge of Old Delhi near Delhi Gate. There's a kitchen, bar, dorms and private rooms.

*For a key to hotel price categories see p114*

### YMCA
MAP F7 ■ Jai Singh Road, Connaught Place ■ 4364 4000 ■ www.new delhiymca.in/hostels ■ ₹
Since 1927, the YMCA hostel has provided excellent budget accommodation for foreign and local visitors. The rooms are basic but clean and have en-suite bathrooms. There is an Internet café and a restaurant serving traditional Indian food.

## B&Bs and Guesthouses

### Dawar Villa B&B
MAP G7 ■ 50 Todarmal Road, Bengali Market ■ 99113 21555 ■ ₹
This smart, family-run B&B is situated in Bengali Market, which is famous for its lively restaurants. Dawar Villa is also close to Mandi House, one of the city's main cultural centres. The place has a warm feel to it, with gorgeous wood panelling, earthy colours and soft lighting.

### Delhi Bed and Breakfast
MAP X1 ■ A-6 Friends Colony (East) ■ 98110 57103 ■ www.delhi bedandbreakfast. com ■ ₹
Featuring bright, quirky furniture, potted plants and wall-hangings, Delhi Bed and Breakfast is a pleasant place to stay. Pervez and Lubna Hameed, the owners, are well travelled, speak fluent French and also offer advice on sight-seeing in the city. Guests are welcome to watch the hostess prepare Indian meals.

### Master Bed and Breakfast
MAP B5 ■ R-500 New Rajendra Nagar ■ 2874 1089 ■ https://masterbed andbreakfast.com ■ ₹
The family who run this beautifully kept little guesthouse are a mine of information on the city and their home is a delight. Breakfast is included and vegetarian meals are available.

### On the House
MAP V1 ■ B-4/120 Safdarjung Enclave ■ 98110 47414 ■ https:// onthehousedelhi.com ■ ₹
This B&B has seven rooms, named after trees, and each is decorated in vivid colours. It prides itself on its homely feel, and the home-cooked food here is delicious. It is a favourite with solo women travellers.

### Sai Villa B&B
MAP W2 ■ E-578 Greater Kailash II ■ 98110 69943 ■ www.saivilla.com ■ ₹
It may not be the most stylish of guesthouses, but Sai Villa offers clean, spacious rooms, well-equipped, en-suite bathrooms, attentive staff and a prime location. The B&B also has deals with a number of nearby restaurants, so guests can ask to have meals delivered to their door.

### Saket B&B
MAP V3 ■ 3rd Floor, D-21 Saket ■ 95828 72580 ■ ₹
Located within a walking distance to the metro station and a short distance from Qutb Minar, Saket B&B is a comfortable option with spacious, well-maintained rooms and en-suite bathrooms.

The popular malls Select Citywalk and DLF Place Saket are also easily accessible from here.

### Tree of Life
MAP V3 ■ D-193 Saket ■ 98102 77699 ■ www. tree-of-life.in ■ ₹
There are seven spotless, spacious rooms, along with a lounge and kitchen, at this friendly little guesthouse in a quiet neighbourhood near the Qutb Minar, a short walk from Saket metro station.

### Trendy B&B
MAP R7 ■ 9-B Mathura Road, Jangpura ■ 98100 19060 ■ www.trendybb. com ■ ₹
Situated close to the Nizamuddin metro station, this B&B has a cosmopolitan feel. The owner is well-travelled and has a network of friends across the globe. The rooms are spotlessly clean and spacious.

### Vandana's B&B
MAP V1 ■ B-4/124 Safdarjung Enclave ■ 93129 42834 ■ ₹
This warm, cosy family-run B&B has a charming rooftop garden, perfect for breakfast in the winter sun or a chilled drink in the summer.

### Eleven
MAP S6 ■ 11 Nizamuddin (East) ■ 98110 88966 ■ www.elevendelhi.com ■ ₹₹
Set in an elegant colonial bungalow with a lawn, the rooms are charming, elegantly furnished and uncluttered. The area is smart, peaceful, quiet and close to several heritage monuments such as the grand Humayun's Tomb.

There is a gym and a mini sports-complex nearby.

## 76 Friends Colony

MAP X1 ▪ 76 Friends Colony (West) ▪ 4145 4681 ▪ www.76friends colonywest.com ▪ ₹₹
This elegant B&B has cosy and well-ventilated rooms with basic amenities. The staff is friendly and helpful. Guests can relax in the lovely terrace garden.

## G 49 Nizamuddin

MAP R6 ▪ G-49 Nizamuddin (West) ▪ 79474 35781 ▪ www. bed-breakfast.asia ▪ ₹₹
Tucked away in a leafy street, this is a relaxed, friendly place with elegant rooms and en-suite bathrooms. The dining area and balcony are lovely places to while away an evening.

## Hotels Around Delhi

### Tiger Den

MAP B3 ▪ Sariska, Alwar ▪ 97846 04323 ▪ email: tigerden.rtdc@ rajasthan.gov.in ▪ ₹
This state-run hotel is a great budget option for visitors to the Sariska Wildlife Sanctuary (see p73). Speak to the staff about sightseeing and safari tours in the park.

### Diggi Palace

MAP B3 ▪ Shivaji Marg, C-Scheme, Jaipur ▪ 0141 236 6120 ▪ www.hotel diggipalace.com ▪ ₹₹
Built around 1727, Diggi Palace is now a heritage hotel situated in the heart of Jaipur. Its fresco painted rooms, grand banquet halls and lush green gardens with

pretty fountains hint at a glorious past. The restaurant serves excellent Rajasthani cuisine.

### Glasshouse on the Ganges

MAP C2 ▪ Village Kalthar, Rishikesh-Badrinath Road, Shivpuri ▪ 0124 4666 166 ▪ www.glassho use-on-the-ganges.neem ranahotels.com ▪ ₹₹₹
Located in a fruit orchard, this hotel has six cottages overlooking the tumbling Ganges. Ask the staff about booking activities such as fishing, trekking and white-water rafting.

### Hill Fort Kesroli

MAP B3 ▪ Kesroli, near MIS Post Office, Bahala, Alwar ▪ 98294 99901 ▪ www.the-hill-fort-kes roli.neemranahotels.com ▪ ₹₹
Set in a 14th-century fort perched on a rocky outcrop, this charming little hotel offers splendid views of the surrounding mustard fields. The rooms are cool, with high ceilings, and are elegantly decorated in traditional style.

### ITC Mughal

MAP C3 ▪ Taj Ganj, Agra ▪ 056 2402 1700 ▪ www. itchotels.com ▪ ₹₹₹
This resort houses the country's largest spa. After a tiring day's sightseeing, relax in a private *hammam* (Turkish bath).

### Kadamb Kunj

MAP C3 ▪ NH 11, Fatehpur Sikri Road, Bharatpur ▪ 97725 80222 ▪ www. kadambkunj.com ▪ ₹
Located not far from the Keoladeo Ghana National Park (see p72), the Kadam Kunj is quite popular with birdwatching enthusiasts.

## Neemrana Fort-Palace

MAP B3 ▪ 122nd Milestone Delhi–Jaipur Highway, Neemrana, Alwar ▪ 0124 466 6166 ▪www.fort-palace.neem ranahotels.com ▪ ₹₹₹
Carved into a hillside, this architectural jewel is steeped in history. Guests can try the pool, which offers amazing views of the countryside, or indulge in rejuvenating Ayurvedic spa treatments.

### The Oberoi Amarvilas

MAP C3 ▪ Taj East Gate Road, Agra ▪ 056 2223 1515 ▪ www.amarvilas. com ▪ ₹₹₹
Constructed in a Moorish- and Mughal-inspired style, this gorgeous five-star property, not far from the Taj Mahal, is a beautiful place to stay.

### Rambagh Palace

MAP B3 ▪ Bhawani Singh Road, Jaipur ▪ 0141 2385 700 ▪ www.tajhotels.com ▪ ₹₹₹
Built in 1835, Rambagh Palace was once the residence of the Maharaja of Jaipur. An elegant air surrounds the lavish grounds of this property, also known as the "Jewel of Jaipur".

### Tikli Bottom

MAP B3 ▪ Gairatpur Baas, PO Tikli, Gurugram ▪ 93133 70853 ▪ www. tiklibottom.com ▪ ₹₹₹
About an hour from Delhi lies this country hotel, owned by former British diplomats who stayed on after their posting in India. A Lutyens-style bungalow built around a courtyard, the house has a swimming pool and an organic farm.

*For a key to hotel price categories see p114*

# General Index

Page numbers in **bold** refer to main entries.

1857 Uprising 13, 15, 43, 57, 84
  monuments of 48–9
1911 65, 79, 82

## A

Abdur Rahim 46, 92
Abu Bakr 49
Accommodation 113, 114–19
Adham Khan's Tomb 26
Adhchini 60
Adiga, Aravinda 56
Adilabad 50
Afghan Wars 20, 77
Agni 79, 82
Agra 7, 69, 73
  hotels 119
  sights 36–7, **38**
  Taj Mahal **36–7**
Agra Fort 17, 38, 73
Agrasen Baoli 80
Air travel 108, 109
Ajmeri Gate 86
Akbar, Emperor 36, 38, 42, 46, 73
  Fatehpur Sikri 39, 73
Akbar Shah II, Emperor 46
Akshara Theatre 62
Akshardham Temple 53, 94, 95
Alai Darwaza (Qutb Minar Complex) 25
Alai Minar (Qutb Minar Complex) 25
Alauddin Khilji, Sultan 25, 43, 44, 45, 50
Ali, Ahmed 57
Aliganj 61
Alwar 73, 119
Amritsar 72
Amrit Udyan 21, 58
Anangpal II, Raja 42, 61
Aqua 65, 79, 82
Arab Serai, The 19
Aravalli Range 48
Architecture, Mughal 47
Ashoka, Emperor 88, 100
Ashoka Column 88
Ashoka's Rock Edict 100

*Asita's Visit to Suddhadhana* (bas-relief) 33
Athpula (Lodi Gardens) 30
Aurangzeb, Emperor 13, 46
Auto rickshaws 69, 106–7, 109
Avalokitesvara 32
Azad, Maulana 16

## B

B&Bs 118–19
Babur, Emperor 19, 30, 42
Bahadur Shah Zafar II, Emperor 43, 85
Baha'i Temple 52, 99, 101
Baker, Herbert 20
Bakr Id 71
Balban's Tomb 26
Ballimaran 66
Baluchari Sari 33
Banerjee, Sarnath 57
Banking 111
Bara Gumbad Masjid 31
Bara Gumbad Tomb 31
Barber's Tomb, The 18
Bars 65
  happy hour 69
  New Delhi 82
  South Delhi 103
Bayly, Christopher 56
Bazaars *see* Markets and bazaars
Beating the Retreat 70
Begum Samru's Palace 15
Begumpuri Masjid 44, 51, 53, 100, 101
Bhai Mati Dass Museum 14
Bharatpur 72, 119
Bhuta Sculpture Gallery (National Crafts Museum) 28
Bijay Mandal 51, 61
Birds *see* Wildlife
Birla, B D 52
Books
  Delhi-inspired 56–7
  shopping 67, 69, 96
Bose, Nandalal 54
Boutique hotels 115–16
British Residency 7, 48
British rule 43
  1857 Uprising 13, 15, 48–9

Bronzes (National Museum) 32, 33, 34
Bu Halima's Garden 19
Buddha Jayanti 71
Buddha Jayanti Park 58
Buddhism, festivals 71
Buddhist art 35
Budget travel
  accommodation 113, 117–18
  tips 69
Buhlul Lodi, Sultan 45
Bukhara 65, 97
Burj-i-Shamali (Red Fort) 13
Bus travel 108, 109

## C

Cafés
  New Delhi 82
  South of Centre 97
  South Delhi 103
Calligraphy, Taj Mahal 36
Car Parts Bazaar 67
Cemeteries *see* Tombs
Central Vista Project 21
Chandni Chowk 6, 10, **14–15**, 85, 87
Change of Guard 68
Charbagh (Taj Mahal) 36
Chauburji Masjid 88
Chawri Bazaar 67, 87
Chhattarpur Mandir 61
China Kitchen, The 65, 105
Chini-ka-Rauza (Agra) 38
Chiragh Delhi 101
Chor Bizarre 64, 89
Chowk-i-Jilo Khana (Taj Mahal) 36
Churches
  Cathedral Church of the Redemption 20, 80
  Central Baptist Church 15
  St James' Church 7, 49, 52, 85
  St Martin's Church 80
Cirrus 9 65, 103
Cities of Delhi 50–51
City Palace (Jaipur) 73
Clothing
  bespoke suits 69, 81
  shopping 81, 96, 102
Concerts, free 68

Connaught Place 7, 67, 77, 79
Coronation Park 59
Correa, Charles 28
Crafts
  shopping 29, 81, 96, 102, 113
  Surajkund Crafts Mela 70
Currency 111
Customs regulations 110
Cycle rickshaws 109

**D**

Dalai Lama 60
Dalrymple, William 57
Dance 62–3, 71
Dancing Girl (bronze) 32
Daniell, Thomas 54
Dara Shikoh, Prince 32, 48
Dargah Qutb Sahib 26–7
Dariba Kalan 66
Daryaganj Sunday Book Market 67
Daulaltabad 42, 51
Daulat Khana (Fatehpur Sikri) 39
Deeg 72
Delhi Comic Con 71
Delhi Sultanate 42
  sights 44–5
Deol, Abhay 57
Desai, Anita 56
Design features, Mughal 47
Dhabas 69
Dilli Haat 67, 96, 113
Dining 113
Disabled travellers 111
Diwali 71
Diwan-i-Aam (Fatehpur Sikri) 39
Diwan-i-Aam (Red Fort) 13, 90–91
Diwan-i-Khas (Fatehpur Sikri) 39
Diwan-i-Khas (Red Fort) 13
Dussehra 66, 71

**E**

Electrical appliances 112
Emergency Services 110–11
Entertainment 62–3
  bars and nightclubs 65
Excursions 72–3

**F**

Fatehpur Sikri 7, 36, **39**, 69, 73
Fatehpuri Masjid 6, 15, 48, 87
Feroz Shah Kotla 45, 51, 88
Feroz Shah Tughlaq, Sultan 45, 50, 51, 88
Ferozabad 45, 51
Festivals and events 70–71
Films
  Delhi in 57
  free 68
Fio Cookhouse & Bar 65, 105
Flagstaff Tower 48
Food and drink
  budget tips 69
  health 110
  places to eat 64–5, 113
  see also Restaurants
Forts
  Adilabad 50
  Agra Fort 17, 38, 73
  Alwar Fort 73
  Purana Qila 46, 51, 71, 93, 97
  Red Fort 10, **12–13**, 47, 85, 87
  Salimgarh Fort 13
  Tughlaqabad 45, 50, 101
Fraser, William 85
Free attractions 68–9
Frykenberg, R E 56

**G**

G-Bar 65
Gandhara kingdom 34
Gandhi, Indira 43, 55, 59, 78, 85
Gandhi, Mohandas K 43
  Gandhi Smriti 6, 7, 55, 68, 79
  National Gandhi Museum 54, 68, 88
  Raj Ghat 59, 85
Gandhi, Rajiv 55, 59, 85
Ganesh Chaturthi 71
Ganga (statue) 32
Gardens see Parks and gardens
Gauri Shankar Mandir 6, 15, 88
George V, King 59

Ghalib, Mirza 43, 88, 95
Ghantewala 15
Ghiyasuddin Tughlaq, Sultan 44, 45, 50
Guliyan Bazaar 66
Gupta, Narayani 56
Gupta Dynasty 34
Gurgaon (Gurugram) 51, 119
Guru Purab 71
Gurudwara Bangla Sahib 52, 69, 80
Gurudwara Sisganj 14
Guesthouses 118–19
Gyms, open-air 68

**H**

Haldiram's 87, 89, 113
Halwa 15
Hanuman Mandir 80
Har Krishnan, Guru 54
Hauz Khas Deer Park 58, 69, 101
Hauz Khas Village 44, 50, 67, 69, 100, 101
  shopping 113
Hauzwali Mosque 88
Hawa Mahal (Jaipur) 73
Hayat Bakhsh Bagh (Red Fort) 12
Health 110, 111
Hinduuism
  festivals 71
  see also Temple, Hindu
Hiran Minar (Fatehpur Sikri) 39
History 42–3
Hodson, William 49
Holi 71
Hostels 117–18
Hotels 113, 114–19
  around Delhi 119
  boutique 115–16
  budget 117–18
  luxury 114–15
  mid-range 116–17
House of Ming 65, 83
House of the Turkish Sultana (Fatehpur Sikri) 39
Humayun, Emperor 19, 46, 51, 93
Humayun's Tomb 10, **18–19**, 46, 74–5, 95
  itineraries 6, 7, 95

**I**

Ibrahim Lodi, Sultan 30, 42
IIC Experience, The 71
Iltutmish, Sultan 24, 25, 45, 99
Immigration 110
Independence 43
India Gate 6–7, 10, 20, 77, 79
India Habitat Centre 63
India International Centre 63, 71
Indian Accent 64, 97
Indus Valley Civilization 11, 32, 34, 54, 77
Indira Gandhi Memorial Museum 55, 68, 78
Indo-Pakistan conflict (1971) 20
Indraprastha 50, 51
Insurance 110
International Mango Festival 70
Internet 112, 113
Iron Pillar 24
Itimad-ud-Daulah (Agra) 38, 73
Itineraries
  A Day in New Delhi 79
  A Day in Old Delhi 87
  A Day South of the Centre of Delhi 95
  A Day in South Delhi 101
  Four Days in Delhi 6–7
  places to eat 89
  Two Days in Delhi 6

**J**

Jahanara, Princess 53
Jahangir, Emperor 46
Jahanpanah 51, 53, 69
Jahaz Mahal 27, 100
Jai Singh II, Maharaja 78
Jaipur 73, 119
Jama Masjid 10, **16–17**, 22–3, 46, 53, 86
  itineraries 6, 7, 87
Jama Masjid (Agra) 38
Jama Masjid (Dargah Mosque) (Fatehpur Sikri) 39
Jamali-Kamali Masjid and Tomb 26, 47, 100
Janpath Market 67
Jantar Mantar 7, 78, 79

Jewellery 81, 96, 102
Jodhabai's Palace (Fatehpur Sikri) 39

**K**

Kalan Masjid 60
Kali (bronze) 33
Kamani Auditorium 62
Kanwarji's 87
Karim's 7, 65, 87, 89
Kartavya Path 6–7, 10, **20–21**, 78, 79
Kashmiri Gate 6, 49, 86
Katra Neel 67
Keoladeo Ghana National Park 72
Khair ul Manazil Masjid 95
Khan, Imran 57
Khan Market 67, 79
Khan-i-Jahan Junan Shah 60
Khan-i-Khanan Tomb 46, 92
Khari Baoli 6, 66, 87, 113
Khas Mahal (Red Fort) 12
Khirki Masjid 45, 101
Khizr Khan, Sultan 30, 45
Khurrana, Ayushmann 57
Khusrau, Amir 53, 95
Kinari Bazaar 66
Kinari Bazaar (Agra) 38
Kitty Su 65
Kizr Sultan 49
Krishen, Pradip 56
Krishna Janmashtami 71
Kushan art 34

**L**

Lahori Gate (Red Fort) 13
Lakshmi Narayan Mandir 52, 79
Lal Darwaza 49
Lal Gumbad 44, 101
Lal Kot 42, 50
Lal Mandir 6, 14, 53, 87
Lala Chunna Mal's Haveli 15
LGBTQ+ 110
Literature 56–7
Lodi Dynasty 30, 44, 45, 58, 93
Lodi Gardens 11, **30–31**, 44, 58, 93
  itineraries 6, 7, 95
  open-air gym 68
  restaurant 31, 95
Lotus Pool (Taj Mahal) 36

Lotus Temple 52, 99
Lutyens, Edwin 20, 21, 43, 51
  Amrit Udyan 58
  India Gate 77
  Kartavya Path 78
  Rashtrapati Bhavan 21, 78, 79
Luxury hotels 114–15

**M**

Madhi Masjid 26
Madrasa of Alauddin Khilji 25
Magazine 49
Maha Shivarati 71
Manju ka Tila 60
Mariam's Tomb (Agra) 38
Markets and bazaars
  Ballimaran 66
  bazaars of Old Delhi 66–7, 86
  Car Parts Bazaar 67
  Chawri Bazaar 67, 87
  Dariba Kalan 66
  Daryaganj Sunday Book Market 67
  Guliyan Bazaar 66
  Janpath Market 67
  Katra Neel 67
  Khan Market 67, 79
  Khari Baoli 6, 66, 87, 113
  Kinari Bazaar 66
  Kinari Bazaar (Agra) 38
  Meena Bazaar 16, 67
  Nai Sarak 66
Masjid see Mosques
Mathura 72
Maurya Empire 34–5
Mausoleums see Tombs
Medd, Henry 20
Meena Bazaar 16, 67
Mehman Khana (Taj Mahal) 37
Mehra, Rakeysh Omprakash 57
Mehrauli Archaeological Park 7, 27, 68, 100, 101
Mehrauli Village 99, 101
  festivals 71
  sites around **26–7**
Mehtab Bagh (Agra) 38
Metcalfe, Sir Thomas 26, 27, 85
Metcalfe's Folly 27
Metro 69, 108, 109
Military parades 21

Miller, Sam 56
Miniature paintings 34, 35
Mirza Ghalib Haveli 88
Mirza Mughal 49
Monkey Bar 65, 103
Mosques
  Bara Gumbad Masjid 31
  Begumpuri Masjid 44, 51,
    53, 100, 101
  Chauburji Masjid 88
  Fatehpuri Masjid 6, 15,
    48, 87
  Hauzwali Mosque 88
  Jama Masjid 10, **16–17**,
    22–3, 46, 53, 86
  Jama Masjid (Agra) 38
  Jama Masjid (Dargah
    Mosque) (Fatehpur Sikri)
    39
  Jamali-Kamali Masjid 26,
    47, 100
  Kalan Masjid 60
  Khair ul Manazil Masjid 95
  Khirki Masjid 45, 101
  Madhi Masjid 26
  Masjid Mubarak Begum 60
  Mosque (Taj Mahal) 37
  Mosque and Tomb of Isa
    Khan 18
  Moti Masjid (Red Fort) 12
  Pataudi House Mosque 17
  Quwwat-ul-Islam 24, 45,
    99
  Sunehri Masjid 15
  Zinat ul Masjid 46, 52, 86
Mosquitoes 110
Moti Masjid (Red Fort) 12
Mughal Dynasty 42
  miniature paintings 35
  Red Fort 13
  sights 46–7
*Mughal Emperor Shah Jahan
  in Dara Shikoh's Marriage
  Procession* 32
Muhammad bin Tughlaq,
  Sultan 42, 43, 45, 53
  Bijay Mandal 51, 61
Muhammad Ghori 24, 42
Muhammad Shah's Tomb 30
Mumtaz Mahal 36
Museums and galleries
  54–5
  Bhai Mati Dass Museum 14
  free entry 68
  Gandhi Smriti 6, 7, 55,
    68, 79

Museums and galleries
  (cont.)
  Indira Gandhi Memorial
    Museum 55, 68, 78
  National Crafts Museum
    11, **28–9**, 54, 68, 79
  National Gallery of
    Modern Art (NGMA) 54,
    68, 80
  National Gandhi Museum
    54, 68
  National Museum 6, 7,
    11, **32–5**, 54, 77, 79
  National Philatelic
    Museum 54, 68, 80
  National Rail Museum
    54, 95
  Pradhanmantri
    Sangrahalaya 55, 68, 80
  Shankar's International
    Dolls Museum 60
  Sulabh International
    Museum of Toilets 55, 68
Music
  festivals 71
  forms of Indian classical
    63
  free concerts 68
  performing arts venues
    62–3
  shopping 81
Muslims 43
  festivals 71
  *see also* Mosques
Mutiny Monument 48

**N**
Nadir Shah 15
Nai Sarak 66
Naidu, Sarojini 43
Nair, Mira 57
Naqqar Khana (Red Fort) 12
Nasiruddin Mahmud, Prince
  99
National Bonsai Garden 30
National Crafts Museum 11,
  **28–9**, 54, 79, 113
  free entry 68
  itineraries 6, 7, 79
National Gallery of Modern
  Art (NGMA) 54, 68, 80
National Gandhi Museum
  54, 68, 88
National Museum 11, **32–5**,
  54, 77
  itineraries 6, 7, 79

National Philatelic Museum
  54, 68, 80
National Rail Museum 54, 95
National School of Drama
  62
  festivals 70
National War Memorial **21**,
  77
National Zoological Park 93
Nativity Painting, Mughal 33
Nehru, Jawaharlal 55, 59,
  85
Nehru Park 59, 68
New Delhi 43, 51, 76–83
  A Day in New Delhi 79
  bars and cafés 82
  map 76–7
  places to eat 83
  shopping 81
  sights 77–80
Newspapers 112, 113
Nicholson, Brigadier-
  General John 49
Nicholson's Cemetery 6,
  49, 88
Nightclubs 65
Nila Gumbad 19
Nizamuddin 40–41, 46,
  52–3, 94–5
  itineraries 6, 7
  music 63
  *qawwalis* 69
Noida 51
Northern Ridge 48, 84, 88
Nur Jahan 38

**O**
Ochterlony, Sir David 60
Off the beaten track 60–61
Oh! Calcutta 101, 104
Old Delhi 42, 50–51, 84–9
  A Day in Old Delhi 87
  bazaars 66–7, 86
  map 84
  places to eat 89
  sights 85–8
Olive Bar & Kitchen 64,
  101, 105
On Foot 109
Opening hours 112

**P**
Pachisi Court (Fatehpur
  Sikri) 39
Paharganj Christian
  Cemetery 61

Palaces
Begum Samru's Palace 15
Bijay Mandal 51, 61
City Palace (Jaipur) 73
Deeg Palace 72
Feroz Shah Kotla 45, 51
Hawa Mahal (Jaipur) 73
Jahaz Mahal 27, 100
Jodhabai's Palace
(Fatehpur Sikri) 39
Panch Mahal (Fatehpur
Sikri) 39
Zafar Mahal 27, 46–7, 100
Panch Mahal (Fatehpur
Sikri) 39
Panipat, Battle of 42
Parks and gardens 58–9
Amrit Udyan 21, 58
Arab Serai, The 19
Bu Halima's Garden 19
Buddha Jayanti Park 58
Charbagh (Taj Mahal) 36
Coronation Park 59
Garden of Five Senses 58,
101
Hauz Khas Deer Park 58
Hayat Bakhsh Bagh (Red
Fort) 12
Humayun's Tomb gardens
18
Lodi Gardens 6, 7, 11,
**30–31**, 44, 58, 93
Mehrauli Archaeological
Park 7, 27, 68
Mehtab Bagh (Agra) 38
National Bonsai Garden 30
Nehru Park 59, 68
Qudsia Bagh 58, 88
Raj Ghat 59
Rambagh Gardens 38
Talkatora Gardens 58, 70
Passports 110, 111
Pataudi House Mosque 17
PCO 65, 103
Perch 95, 97
Performing arts venues 62–3
Personal security 110–11
Phool Walon ki Sair 71
Pietra dura 37, 47
Pir Ghaib 88
Police 111
Places of Worship 52–3
Postal services 112, 113
Prager, Dave 56
Prithviraj Chauhan III, King
42

Puppets 62
Purana Qila 46, 51, 71, 93
itineraries 6, 7, 95

**Q**
Q'BA 79, 82
Qila Rai Pithora 50
Qudsia Bagh 6, 58, 88
Quli Khan's Tomb 26, 27
Qutb Festival 71
Qutb Minar Complex 11,
**24–5**, 44, 99
itineraries 7, 101
Qutbuddin Aibak, Sultan
24, 42, 43, 45, 99
Quwwat-ul-Islam 24, 45, 99

**R**
Radio 112, 113
Rail travel 108, 109
Raisina Hill 20, 21
Raj Ghat 59, 85
Rajon ki Bain 26
Rama Navami 71
Rambagh Gardens (Agra) 38
Rang Mahal (Red Fort) 13
Rani Lakshmibai of Jhansi
43
Rashtrapati Bhavan 10, 21,
51, 78
itineraries 7, 79
Razia Sultan 43, 45, 87
Red Fort 10, **12–13**, 47, 85
itineraries 6, 87
Religious festivals 71
Republic Day Parade 21, 70
Restaurants 64–5, 113
New Delhi 83
Old Delhi 89
set menus 69
South of the Centre 97
South Delhi 104–5
Road travel 108–9
Round Tower (Lodi Gardens)
31
Rick's 65, 82
Russell, Robert Tor 77

**S**
Sabz Burj 19
Safdarjung's Tomb 6, 7, 47,
94, 95
Safety
personal security 110, 111
travel safety advice 110,
111

Salimgarh Fort 13
Sangeet Natak Akademi
62
Sansad Bhavan 20, 79, 80
Santushti 67
Saravana Bhavan 64, 83
Sariska Tiger Reserve 73
Sarojini Nagar 67
Satellite cities 51
Sayyid dynasty 30, 44, 45,
58, 93
Secretariat Buildings 20,
51, 80
Select Citywalk Complex 67
Shah Jahan, Emperor 14,
38, 42, 43, 84
Jama Masjid 17, 46
master builder 17
painting of 32
Red Fort 12, 13
Shahjahanabad 51
Taj Mahal 36, 37
Shahi Burj (Red Fort) 13
Shahpur Jat Market 102
Shajahanabad 12, 42, 51
Shankar's International
Dolls Museum 60
Sher Shah Suri 19, 43, 51, 93
Shish Gumbad 31
Shiva Nataraja (bronze) 33,
77
Shopping 112, 113
bazaars of old Delhi 66–7
crafts 29
New Delhi 81
shops and markets 67
South of the Centre 96
South Delhi 102
see also Markets and
bazaars
Shri Ram Centre for
Performing Arts 62
Sikandar Lodi, Sultan 36,
45
Sikander Lodi's Tomb 30
Sikandra (Agra) 38
Sikhs 43
festivals 71
see also Temples, Sikh
Singh, Khushwant 56–7
Siri 44, 50
Siri Fort Cultural Complex
63
Skinner, Colonel James 52,
85
Social 65, 103

SodaBottleOpenerWala 64, 79, 97
South of the Centre 92–7
  A Day South of the Centre of Delhi 95
  map 92–3
  places to eat 97
  shopping 96
  sights 92–5
South Delhi 98–103
  A Day in South Delhi 101
  bars and cafés 103
  map 98–9
  places to eat 104–5
  shopping 102
  sights 99–101
Spear, Percival 56
Special needs 111
Spice Route 64, 83
State Emporia Complex 67, 81, 113
Stepwells (baoli) 26, 80
Sulabh International Museum of Toilets 55, 68
Sultanpur Bird Sanctuary 72
Sultans 45
Sunder Nursery 58
Sunehra Makan (Fatehpur Sikri) 39
Sunehri Masjid 15
Surajkund Crafts Mela 70
Surajkund Dam 61
Swaminarayan, Bhagwan Shri 53
Sweets 15, 87

**T**
Tailors 69, 81
Taj Mahal (Agra) 7, 8–9, 11, **36–7**, 73
Taj Nature Walk (Agra) 38
Talkatora Gardens 58, 70
Tarain, Battle of 42
Tavernier, Jean-Baptiste 37
Taxis 108–9
Tea 69, 96
Telephone services 112, 113
Television 112, 113
Temples, Hindu
  Akshardham Temple 53, 94, 95
  Chhatarpur Mandir 61
  free entry 69
  Gauri Shankar Mandir 6, 15, 88

Temples, Hindu (cont.)
  Hanuman Mandir 80
  Lakshmi Narayan Mandir 52, 79
Temples, Jain, Lal Mandir 6, 14, 53, 87
Temples, Sikh
  Golden Temple (Amritsar) 72
  Gurudwara Bangla Sahib 52, 69, 80
  Gurudwara Sisganj 14
Textiles
  National Museum 35
  shopping 81, 96, 102
  Textile Gallery (National Crafts Museum) 29
Theatre 62–3, 71
Tibetan colony 60, 113
Tickets, discount 69
Time management 112
Timur 30, 42
Tomar Dynasty 42, 50
Tombs
  Adham Khan's Tomb 26
  Balban's Tomb 26
  Bara Gumbad Tomb 31
  Barber's Tomb, The 18
  Chini-ka-Rauza (Agra) 38
  Humayun's Tomb 10, **18–19**, 46, 74–5, 95
  Itimad-ud-Daulah (Agra) 38, 73
  Jamali-Kamali Tomb 26
  Khan-i-Khanan Tomb 46, 92
  Lal Gumbad 44, 101
  Mariam's Tomb (Agra) 38
  Muhammad Shah's Tomb 30
  Nicholson's Cemetery 6, 49, 88
  Nila Gumbad 19
  Nizamuddin 40–41, 46, 52–3, 94–5
  Paharganj Christian Cemetery 61
  Quli Khan's Tomb 26, 27
  Sabz Burj 19
  Safdarjung's Tomb 6, 7, 47, 94, 95
  Shish Gumbad 31
  Sikander Lodi's Tomb 30
  Sikandra (Agra) 38
  Taj Mahal (Agra) 7, 8–9, 11, **36–7**, 73

Tombs (cont.)
  Tomb of Ghiyasuddin Tughlaq 44
  Tomb of Iltutmish 25
  Tomb of Imam Zamin 24
  Tomb of Isa Khan 18
  Tomb of Maulana Azad 16
  Tomb of Razia Sultan 87
  Tomb of Sultan Ghari 99
  Tomb of the Unknown Soldier 20, 77
Town Hall 14
Travel 108–9
  budget tips 69
  safety advice 110, 111
Travellers with Specific Needs 111
Trees 59
Trips and tours 112, 113
Triveni Kala Sangam 62
Triveni Tea Terrace 79, 82
Tughlaq Dynasty 42, 44
Tughlaqabad 45, 50, 101
Turkman, Hazrat Shah 86, 87
Turkman Gate 86, 87

**V**
Vaccinations 110
Vegetarians 113
Vijay Chowk 21, 70
Vintage Car Rally 70
Visas 110, 111
Visitor information 112, 113
Vrindavan 72

**W**
Water, drinking 110
Weather 112
Wildlife
  Hauz Khas Deer Park 58, 69, 101
  Lodi Gardens birdlife 31
  National Zoological Park 93
  Sariska Tiger Reserve 73
  Sultanpur Bird Sanctuary 72
World War I 20, 77

**Z**
Zafar Mahal 27, 46–7, 100
Zinat ul Masjid 46, 52, 86

# Acknowledgments

## This edition updated by

**Contributor** Madhavi Singh
**Senior Editor** Alison McGill
**Senior Designer** Stuti Tiwari
**Project Editor** Anuroop Sanwalia
**Assistant Editors** Abhidha Lakhera, Anjasi N.N., Vineet Singh
**Picture Research Manager** Taiyaba Khatoon
**Picture Research Administrator** Vagisha Pushp
**Publishing Assistant** Simona Velikova
**Jacket Designer** Jordan Lambley
**Cartography Manager** Suresh Kumar
**Cartographer** Ashif
**Senior DTP Designer** Tanveer Zaidi
**Senior Production Editor** Jason Little
**Production Controller** Kariss Ainsworth
**Managing Editors** Shikha Kulkarni, Beverly Smart, Hollie Teague
**Managing Art Editor** Sarah Snelling
**Senior Managing Art Editor** Priyanka Thakur
**Art Director** Maxine Pedliham
**Publishing Director** Georgina Dee

DK would like to thank the following for their contribution to the previous editions:
Gavin Thomas, Janice Pariat, Avantika Sukhia, Clare Peel, Helen Peters

The publisher would like to thank the following for their kind permission to reproduce their photographs:
**Key:** a-above; b-below/bottom; c-centre; f-far; l-left; r-right; t-top

**123RF.com:** Sergey Belov 18bl; Lukasz Nowak 17crb; saiko3p 79cla.

**Alamy Stock Photo:** Arterra Picture Library 2tl, 2tr, 8–9, 40–1; Anders Blomqvist 32crb; dbimages 10cra, 26t, 34br, 69tr, 76tl, 99br; Deco 4t; Hemis 3tr, 55br, 94br, 106–7; Angelo Hornak 32ca, 33tl, 33br; imageBROKER 61tr, 77tl; Inge Johnsson 4crb; Seth Lazar 27r; Stelios Michael 49tr; MJ Photography 14br; William Mullins 4cla; Panther Media GmbH / Joerg Hackemann / meinzahn 67bl; David Pearson 13crb; PhotosIndia.com LLC 60cbl; Graham Prentice 22–3; Pep Roig 16bl; Tjetjep Rustandi 12–3; SOPA Images Limited 10cb; travelib prime 88cla; Xinhua 71tr; ZUMA Press; Inc. 57tr / Ravi Batra 4cl.

**Amrapali:** 96ca.

**AWL Images:** Kav Dadfar 1**;** Gavin Hellier 53clb; Hemis 37crb; Nigel Pavitt 13tl; Jane Sweeney 4cr.

**Chirag Bariya:** 104tr.

**Subhadeep Biswas:** 11cr, 30cla, 30–1, 45cl.

**Dreamstime.com:** Stuart Atkinson 39cb; Atosan 11tc, 66cbl; Viacheslav Belyaev 84tl, 93tr; Ajay Bhaskar 78tl, 101cl; Byelikova 73b, 85b; Mike Clegg 10cla; Donyanedomam 38b; Eermakova 90–1; Elenatur 36–7; Euriico 80bl; Monica Furlong 11br; Jorg Hackemann 10clb, 19crb, 47tr; Attila Jandi 73cra; Javiphotos 94t; Kajornyot 72c; Mdsindia 54br; Meinzahn 4clb; Mvorobiev 50b; Moreno Novello 100b; Paweł Opaska 39t; William Perry 30crb; Marina Pissarova 58tl; Luca Roggero 59cl; Dmitry Rukhlenko 6cla; Saiko3p 16–7, 36cla, 44b, 51t, 55t, 52t, 61b, 77br, 78b; Sergeychernov 46–7; Dr Ajay Kumar Singh 59tr; Singhsomendra 67tr; Pavalache Stelian 37tl; Rudolf Tepfenhart 38cla; Westhimal 7cra; Yuri Yavnik 7tr; Yurataranik 72tl, 98cla; Zatletic 53br.

**Fabindia:** 102cr.

**FIO Cookhouse and Bar:** 105br.

**Getty Images:** Emad Aljumah 24–5, 85tr; Mukul Banerjee Photography 3tl, 47clb, 74–5; Bettmann 43br; Anders Blomqvist 29bl; Bloomberg 104cb; Education Images 20cla; Hindustan Times 48t, 62t; Angelo Hornak 11clb, 35bc, 42cr; Hulton Archive / Keystone 43cla; IndiaPictures 32clb, 33bl, 35cl, 63tr; JUST LIKE THAT! 44tl, 88bc, 92cla; Ramesh Lalwani 52clb; LightRocket / SOPA Images / Naveen Sharma 70t; Mail Today 97tr; Maremagnum 66tr; Patrick McMullan 56tl; Mint 64b; Ashu Mittal 70bc; Moment / Neha Gupta 20bl; Pacific Press 62cb; Christine Pemberton 48bl; Christopher Pillitz 68br; Rhkamen 29tl; Smit Sandhir 27cb; Mohan Singh 14cla, 15br; Leisa Tyler 65cla; Manan Vatsyayana 58–9; Visuals Unlimited; Inc. / Adam Jones 31tr.

**Getty Images / iStock:** amlanmathur 51br; Anton Aleksenko 12bl; Pradeep Gaur 4b; Jayesh 25clb; JDMaddox 31bc; Alan Lagadu 87tl; Meinzahn 18–9; Harjeet Singh Narang 17c, 68t; Soumen Nath 18cla; P_A_S 21bl; powerofforever 25tl; Saiko3p 24cla; Arnav Pratap Singh 20-21c; SoumenNath 46tl.

**Kingshuk Ghoshal:** 71clb.

**Good Earth:** 96b.

**Indian Accent:** Rohit Chawla 64ca.

**National Railway Museum, India:** photo Dorling Kindersley Ltd/Deepak Aggarwal 95cl.

**Old World Hospitality Pvt. Ltd.:** 89cr.

**PCO Bar:** 103b.

**Penguin Random House India:** *Delhi: Adventures in a Megacity* by Sam Miller 56cb; Cover illustration by Sarnath Banerjee 57bl.

**Robert Harding Picture Library:** Peter Barritt 45br.

**Shutterstock.com:** meunierd 10b.

**Sulabh International Museum of Toilets:** 55c.

**The Park New Delhi:** 65br, 82t.

**The Shop:** 81cla.

**The Taj Mahal Hotel, New Delhi:** 83crb.

#### Cover

Front and spine: **AWL Images:** Kav Dadfar.

Back: **Alamy Stock Photo:** Jon Arnold Images Ltd crb, TMI cla**; AWL Images:** Kav Dadfar b**; Dreamstime.com:** Yuri Yavnik tr**; Getty Images / iStock:** mariusz_prusaczyk tl.

#### Pull Out Map Cover
**AWL Images:** Kav Dadfar.

All other images © Dorling Kindersley
For further information see:
www.dkimages.com

**Commissioned Photography** Idris Ahmed, Dinesh Khanna

Penguin
Random
House

First edition 2010

Published in Great Britain by
Dorling Kindersley Limited
DK, One Embassy Gardens, 8 Viaduct
Gardens, London SW11 7BW, UK

The authorised representative in the EEA is
Dorling Kindersley Verlag GmbH. Arnulfstr.
124, 80636 Munich, Germany

Published in the United States by
DK Publishing, 1745 Broadway, 20th Floor,
New York, NY 10019, USA

Copyright © 2010, 2023 Dorling
Kindersley Limited
A Penguin Random House Company

23 24 25 26 10 9 8 7 6 5 4 3 2 1

A CIP catalogue record is available
from the British Library.

A catalogue record for this book is available
from the Library of Congress.

ISSN 1479-344X

ISBN 978-0-2416-2502-6

Printed and bound in Malaysia

www.dk.com

*As a guide to abbreviations in visitor information
blocks:* **Adm** = admission charge.

**MIX**
Paper | Supporting
responsible forestry

**FSC™ C018179**

This book was made with Forest
Stewardship Council™ certified
paper – one small step in DK's
commitment to a sustainable future.
**For more information go to
www.dk.com/our-green-pledge**

# Selected Street Index

| | |
|---|---|
| Africa Avenue | U1 |
| Ajmal Khan Road | D3 |
| Ajmeri Gate Road | G4 |
| Akbar Road | M5 |
| Alaknanda Badarpur Road | W3 |
| Amrita Shergill Marg | N5 |
| Anuvrat Marg | U3 |
| Arab Ki Sarai Road | S6 |
| Aruna Asaf Ali Marg | U2 |
| Asaf Ali Road | H5 |
| Ashoka Road | N2 |
| Atul Grover Road | P1 |
| August Kranti Marg | V2 |
| Aurangzeb Road | N5 |
| Aurobindo Marg | V2 |
| Azad Market Road | E2 |
| Baba Ganganath Marg | U2 |
| Baba Kharak Singh Marg | E7 |
| Bahadur Shah Zafar Marg | H6 |
| Bahadurgarh Road | E2 |
| Ballimaran | G3 |
| Bangla Sahib Road | E7 |
| Bara Hindu Rao Road | E3 |
| Barakhamba Road | G7 |
| Basant Road | F5 |
| Bazaar Chitli Qabar Marg | H5 |
| Bhagwan Das Road | Q2 |
| Bhai Vir Singh Marg | E7 |
| Bhairon Marg | R3 |
| Bharat Scouts & Guides Marg | R6 |
| Bhav Bhutti Marg | G5 |
| Bhisham Pitamah Marg | P6 |
| Birbal Road | R7 |
| Brassey Avenue | L3 |
| Car Parts Bazaar | G4 |
| Canning Road | P2 |
| Central Golf Link Road | Q6 |
| Chamelian Road | E3 |
| Chandni Chowk | G3 |
| Chandragupta Marg | K5 |
| Chawri Bazaar | G4 |
| Chel Puri | G4 |
| Chelmsford Road | F6 |
| Chirag Delhi Main Road | W2 |
| Church Mission Marg | G3 |
| Church Road | L2 |
| Churi Walan Gali | G4 |
| Connaught Circus | F7 |
| Copernicus Marg | Q2 |
| Dara Shikoh Road | M3 |
| Dariba Kalan | H3 |
| Daulat Ram Marg | F3 |
| Deen Dayal Upadhyaya Marg | H6 |
| Desh Bandhu Gupta Road | F5 |
| Dr Bishambar Das Marg | M1 |
| Dr Rajendra Prasad Road | N2 |
| Dr Zakir Hussain Marg | Q4 |
| Eastern Avenue | X1 |
| Esplanade Road | H4 |
| Feroz Shah Road | P1 |
| Geetanjali Marg | V2 |
| Grand Trunk Road | E1 |
| Guliyan Bazaar | G4 |
| Guru Ravi Das Marg | X3 |
| Gurudwara Rakab Ganj Road | M2 |
| Hailey Road | G7 |
| Hamilton Road | G2 |
| Hanuman Road | N1 |
| Harsha Road | S7 |
| Hindu Rao Marg | F1 |
| Hoshiar Singh Marg | B3 |
| Humayun Road | P4 |
| Idgah Road | E3 |
| Indraprastha Marg | J7 |
| Jai Singh Marg | N1 |
| Janpath | N3 |
| Jantar Mantar Road | N2 |
| Jaswant Singh Road | P2 |
| Jawaharlal Nehru Marg | H5 |
| Jawaharlal Nehru Stadium Marg | Q7 |
| Jhandewalan Road | E4 |
| Jor Bagh Road | N7 |
| Josip Broz Tito Marg | W2 |
| Kachehri Road | F2 |
| Kali Bari Road | D7 |
| Kalindi Kunj Road | Y2 |
| Kamal Ataturk Marg | M6 |
| Kamraj Road | M4 |
| Karnal Road | F2 |
| Kartavya Path | N3 |
| Kasabpur Road | E4 |
| Kasturba Gandhi Marg | P2 |
| Kasturba Hospital Marg | H4 |
| Katra Bariyan | F3 |
| Katra Neel | G3 |
| Kautilya Marg | L5 |
| Khari Baoli | F3 |
| Khel Gaon Marg | V2 |
| Khirki Main Road | V2 |
| Kinari Bazaar | G3 |
| Kotla Marg | H6 |
| Kripa Narayan Marg | G1 |
| Krishna Menon Marg | M4 |
| Lal Bahadur Shastri Road | R6 |
| Lala Hardev Sahai Marg | G2 |
| Lala Lajpat Rai Path | R7 |
| Lalkuan Bazaar Road | G4 |
| Lambi Gali | G4 |
| Liberty Road | E2 |
| Link Road | D5 |
| Lok Kalyan Marg | M5 |
| Lodi Road | P6 |
| Lok Sabha Marg | M2 |
| Lothian Road | G2 |
| Maharaja Aggarsain Marg | F3 |
| Maharaja Ranjeet Singh Marg | G6 |
| Maharishi Balmiki Marg | M2 |
| Maharishi Raman Marg | P5 |
| Mahatma Gandhi Marg | S5 |
| Mahatma Jyoti Rao Phule Road | Q2 |
| Main Bazar Road | E5 |
| Man Singh Road | P3 |
| Mandir Marg | D6 |
| Mathura Road | R4 |
| Maulana Azad Road | N3 |
| Maulana Mohammad Ali Marg | X2 |
| Max Mueller Marg | P6 |
| Meena Bazaar | H4 |
| Mehrauli-Badarpur Road | W3 |
| Mirdard Marg | H6 |
| Moolchand Flyover | W1 |
| More Sarai Road | H3 |
| Mother Teresa Crescent | K2 |
| Motilal Nehru Marg | N4 |
| Munirka Marg | T2 |
| Nai Sarak | G3 |
| Nauroji Nagar Marg | U1 |
| Nawab Road | E3 |
| Naya Bans Bazaar | F3 |
| Naya Bazaar | F3 |
| Nehru Place Road | X2 |
| Nelson Mandela Marg | T2 |
| Netaji Subhash Marg | H4 |
| New Rohtak Road | D3 |
| Nicholson Road | G2 |
| Niti Marg | L6 |
| North Avenue | L2 |
| Nyaya Marg | K6 |
| Outer Ring Road | X2 |
| Panchkuian Road | E5 |
| Panchsheel Marg | K5 |
| Pandara Road | Q4 |
| Pandit Pant Marg | M1 |
| Park Street | L1 |
| Poorvi Marg | T2 |
| Press Enclave Marg | V3 |
| Prithviraj Lane | P5 |
| Prithviraj Road | N5 |
| Purana Qila Road | Q3 |
| Qutab Road | F3 |
| Rafi Ahmed Kidwai Marg | N3 |
| Raisina Hill | M3 |
| Raisina Road | N2 |
| Raj Niwas Marg | F1 |
| Raja Dhirsain Marg | W2 |
| Rajaji Marg | M4 |
| Rajesh Pilot Marg | N5 |
| Rajpur Road | F1 |
| Rajya Sabha Marg | M2 |
| Ram Bagh Road | D2 |
| Rama Krishna Ashram Marg | L1 |
| Rani Jhansi Road | E3 |
| Rao Tula Ram Marg | T1 |
| Ring Road | S4 |
| Road No 13a | Y2 |
| Roshanara Road | E1 |
| Safdarjung Road | M5 |
| Sansad Marg | M2 |
| Sardar Patel Marg | K4 |
| Satya Marg | K7 |
| Satya Sadan | L7 |
| Shaheed Bhagat Singh Marg | E6 |
| Shaheed Jeet Singh Marg | U2 |
| Shah Jahan Road | P4 |
| Sham Nath Marg | G1 |
| Shanti Path | K6 |
| Shershah Road | Q3 |
| Shraddhanand Marg | F4 |
| Shyama Prasad Mukherji Marg | G3 |
| Sikandra Road | Q1 |
| Siri Fort Marg | V2 |
| Sitaram Bazaar Road | G4 |
| South Avenue | L4 |
| Subramaniam Bharti Marg | P5 |
| Swarna Jayanti Marg | F3 |
| Talkatora Road | M2 |
| Tambraparini Marg | R3 |
| Tansen Marg | G7 |
| Teen Murti Marg | M5 |
| Tees January Marg | N5 |
| Thyagaraja Marg | M4 |
| Tilak Marg | Q2 |
| Tolstoy Marg | N1 |
| Tughlaq Road | N5 |
| Turkman Marg | G6 |
| Vandemataram Marg | D5 |
| Vedanta Desika Mandir Marg | U2 |
| Vasant Marg | T1 |
| Vijay Chowk | M3 |
| Vikas Marg | J7 |
| Vinay Marg | L7 |
| Viviekanand Road (Minto Road) | G5 |
| Zoological Park Road | R4 |
| Zorawar Singh Marg | E2 |